STEP FIVE - MULTIPLICATION

TEACHER MANUAL

DR HENDRIK VORSTER

STEP FIVE - MULTIPLICATION

-- Teacher Manual --

"Ephesians 4:12 (NIV)
   "to equip his people for works of service, so that the body of Christ may be built up..."

Dr. Hendrik J Vorster

Discipleship Foundations
Step 5 – Multiplication (Teacher Manual)
By Dr. Hendrik J. Vorster

A practical leadership guide to disciple fruit-producers.

Apart from this Handbook, you will also need the following items to complete your study:
A New International Version of the Bible.
A pen or pencil to write the answers.
Coloured pencils (red, blue, green and yellow).

For more copies and information please visit and write to us at: www. churchplantinginstitute.com

or connect with us at: resources@churchplantinginstitute.com

Scripture taken from the HOLY BIBLE,

New International Version

Copyright 1973, 1978, 1984, 2011 Biblica.

Used by permission of Zondervan.

The Church Planting Doctor and Church Planting Institute are a Registered Ministries of Cornerstone Ministries International.

ISBN 13-978-1-7366426-1-0

INDEX

1

INTRODUCTION

The *goal of Discipleship* is *to become fruitful,* and *to multiply Leaders,* to *advance the Kingdom of God. Jesus* was *quite determined* in *his message to* the *disciples,* when *He outlined His* expectation, about *fruitfulness* in *John chapter 15.*

> *John 15:8 (NIV) 8 This is to my Father's glory, that you bear much fruit, showing yourselves to be my disciples.*

> *John 15:16 (NIV) 16 You did not choose me, but I chose you and appointed you so that you might go and bear fruit —fruit that will last—and so that whatever you ask in my name the Father will give you.*

It *seems,* from this message, *that Jesus directly connects our ability* to *bear fruit,* with *calling ourselves His followers.* One of *our greatest expressions,* of *giving glory* to *our Heavenly Father,* is *by bearing lasting fruit.*

All our *learning, assimilating of values, developing skills,* and *refining our character,* through well-established disciplines, *means little, if it does not produce lasting fruit.*

The Test of Discipleship.

Our goal is to *set up goal posts,* to *keep us focused* on the *real goals: Lasting Fruit.* The *litmus test,* of *true discipleship, is souls* that *follow* in the *footsteps of Jesus.* The *reality check,* for all *our efforts,* is whether *those we pursue,* have *been born again,* and *are on a trajectory of learning: being taught to <u>obey</u> everything Jesus taught us.*

How do we accomplish this?

In the *following lessons* we will *explore* a few *goal posts,* to *keep us focused,* and *on track, to do* what we set out to do, *to fulfil the great Commission,* we received from the Lord.

2

VISION AND DREAMS

U nderstanding *visions and dreams*, are *essential*, in us
fulfilling, God's revealed plans for our lives.

A Vision defines what <u>God</u> plans for us to do.

Understanding the Visions, and dreams God gave us, also *clarifies His expectations* and *outcomes*. One way of clarifying, and understanding the vision of God, is by *writing it down*. Having *a clear vision defines our purpose* and *goals*.

> *Proverbs 29:18 (AMP) "Where there is **no vision** [no redemptive revelation of God], the **people <u>perish</u>**; ...'*

> *Proverbs 29:18 "Where there is **no revelation, the people cast off restraint;"***

The *only way, to not perish,* is to *have,* and *keep, a God-given vision,* alive *in your heart. God has* such *a plan,* and *a Purpose,* for *each one of us.* He declared that *He has such a plan to us,* through the prophetic word in *Jeremiah chapter 29 verse 11.*

*Jeremiah 29:11 (NIV) 11 For **I know the plans I have for you,"** declares the LORD, "**plans to prosper you** and not to harm you, **plans** to give you hope and a future.*

God's plan gives us *a hopeful future*. Understanding God's plan, affirms His Presence, His Provision, and His protection over us.

God's Plan equals God's Vision for our lives.

How do we receive a vision from God?

There are a number of ways to understand a Vision.

- On a *Corporate Level*, a *vision defines the objectives* of a corporation. The *Mission Statement defines, how* they will get *to fulfil their Vision.*
- On a *Personal level*, a *vision* could be, the *pursuit* of a *personal ideal,* such as, *achieving a certain academic level of education,* or *achieving something significant like,* building the *biggest cell group* in *your church.*
- On a *Spiritual level*, a *vision* is something *you pursue, or act on, as a result* of *a divine* revelation.

In this session we are *specifically focused* on understanding the, *how to receive* a *divinely, inspired vision* from God.

As indicated, at the beginning of this session, I believe that *God has a plan, and a purpose,* for *each one of us.* This in essence *defines His Vision* for our lives. *His plan* and purpose *become our vision* to *pursue and fulfill.*

A Vision is received in a number of ways.

Through a Supernatural encounter.

We can *receive* an <u>*open*</u> *vision* through *a Supernatural encounter* with God, as it seems *common* among *many* of the *Biblical Leaders*. An *open vision occurs* when *God reveals Himself*, in the natural, in a moment.

Abraham had open visions from God

God spoke to *Abraham* through *open visions*, both through His initial encounter in Genesis 12, when He called Abraham out of his Father's land, and then again, when He appeared to him in Genesis 15.

> *Genesis 15:1 (NIV) 1 After this, **the word of the LORD** came to Abram **in a vision:** "Do not be afraid, Abram. I am your shield, your very great reward."*

Jacob had open visions from God

God also *spoke* to **Jacob in a Vision** at night.

> *Genesis 46:2 (NIV) 2 And **God spoke** to Israel **in a vision** at night and said, "Jacob! Jacob!" "Here I am," he replied.*

Isaiah had an open vision from God

On a few instances, in the Book of Isaiah, we read of the amazing visions Isaiah had,

> *Isaiah 6:1 (NIV) 1 In the year that King Uzziah died, **I saw the Lord**, high and exalted, seated on a throne; and the train of his robe filled the temple.*

Paul had open visions from God

Another example is that of when *Paul* received his "*Macedonian Call*" in *a Vision at night*. This is a great example of receiving, *a divinely inspired vision* from God, which **outlined His plan** for Paul. It was in following this, Vision from God, that the church in Philippi was launched.

> *Acts 16:9-10 (NIV) 9 **During the night** Paul had **a vision** of a man of Macedonia standing and begging him, "Come over to Macedonia and help us." 10 After Paul had **seen the vision**, we **got ready at once** to leave for Macedonia, **concluding** that God had **called us to preach the gospel** to them.*

Through dreams.

We can **receive a vision,** while we are **sleeping and dreaming**. Abimelek, the King of Gerar, received a message from God **through a dream** during the night, regarding Sarah, that she was indeed Abraham's wife, and that he needed to release her from his pursuit for her affection.

> *Genesis 20:3 (NIV) 3 But **God came to Abimelek in a dream** one night and said to him, "You are as good as dead because of the woman you have taken; she is a married woman."*

Daniel seemed to have **quite a few** of these **visionary dreams**, and we read about these throuhout the Book of Daniel.

> *Daniel 2:19 (NIV) 19 **During the night** the **mystery was revealed to** Daniel **in a vision**. Then Daniel praised the God of heaven."*

From an account in the Book of *Job* we can derive that He was **acquainted** with receiving **visions in dreams** at night.

*Job 33:15 (NIV) 15 **In a dream, in a vision** of the night, when deep
    sleep falls on people as they slumber in their beds,*

Through prayer.

We can also *receive a revelation* from God *through prayer. Daniel* is one
of those who frequently *had visions from God, some* of the *visions* came
during the night in his sleep and others *whilst in prayer*. On this occasion we read that *Daniel was in prayer* when an Angel appeared to
him with a message. The **prophetic message**, of things to happen,
came to Daniel while he was praying. *An Angel of God* brought the
message to him.

*Daniel 9:20-23 (NIV) 20 While **I was speaking and praying**,
    confessing my sin and the sin of my people Israel and making
    my request to the LORD my God for his holy hill — 21 **while I
    was still in prayer, Gabriel, the man I had seen in the earlier
    vision**, came to me in swift flight about the time of the evening
    sacrifice. 22 **He instructed me** and said to me, "Daniel, I have
    now come to give you insight and understanding. 23 As soon as
    you began to pray, a word went out, which I have come to tell
    you, for you are highly esteemed. Therefore, **consider the word
    and understand the vision:***

The *Apostle Peter* is another example of one who received a vision
from *God during prayer*. The vision revealed to him an assignment
that he needed to undertake to Cornelius' house.

*Acts 11:4-7 (NIV) 4 Starting from the beginning, Peter told them the
    whole story: 5 "I was in the city of Joppa praying, and in a
    trance, I saw a vision. I saw something like a large sheet being
    let down from heaven by its four corners, and it came down to
    where I was. 6 I looked into it and saw four-footed animals of
    the earth, wild beasts, reptiles and birds. 7 Then I heard a voice
    telling me, 'Get up, Peter. Kill and eat.'*

Through a Prophetic Word.

We can also *receive God's vision* for our lives through *a prophetic Word* delivered to us. On one occasion *a Prophet came from Jerusalem* to Antioch. *He predicted* through the Holy Spirit that *a severe famine* would spread *throughout* the *Roman world. The result* of this vision that he shared was that *the Believers made a collection to assist* those who would be affected by this future famine.

> *Acts 11:28-30 (NIV) 28 One of them, named Agabus, stood up and through the Spirit predicted that a severe famine would spread over the entire Roman world. (This happened during the reign of Claudius.) 29 The disciples, as each one was able, decided to provide help for the brothers and sisters living in Judea. 30 This they did, sending their gift to the elders by Barnabas and Saul.*

Through an Angelic visitation.

We can *receive* a *vision* from an *Angelic visitation*, such as was the case with *Cornelius* while he was *in prayer*. The Lord told him what to do and he did it. The *result* was that *He and his household received the Word* of God, the *Baptism of the Holy Spirit* and they all *followed* the Lord through the *waters of Baptism*.

> *Acts 10:3 (NIV) 3 One day at about three in the afternoon he had a vision. He distinctly saw an angel of God, who came to him and said, "Cornelius!"*

Through Fasting and Prayer.

Sometimes *visions come during* or after *a period of fasting* and *prayer*. This was the case for *Daniel* after he *fasted* for *three weeks*.

How do we receive this Vision from God?

1. Wait with expectation for the Vision

Wait expectantly for the revelation of God. *Ask the Lord,* for His purpose and plan for your life, and ministry, *to be revealed.*

> *Habakkuk 2:1 (NIV) 1 I will stand at my watch and station myself on the ramparts; I will look to see what he will say to me, and what answer I am to give to this complaint.*

As *part* of your *daily time with God, keep watch to see* what *the Lord might reveal to you,* by His Holy Spirit. *God might bring direct messages to you,* or *through you to others, or to you, through others.* The *"others"* might be *individuals, groups of people* or even for *people in high positions* or *for nations.*

2. Listen to the Voice of the Holy Spirit.

Jesus said that, His *sheep knows His voice,* and *they listen.* I believe the Lord desires, to speak to us daily. We need to be attentive to His voice. He will speak, if He knows we will listen and obey.

> *John 10:27 (NIV) 27 My sheep listen to my voice; I know them, and they follow me.*

The Leaders who gathered in the *Church in Antioch listened,* and *acted* ,when the *Holy Spirit spoke* to them about the *work assigned* for *Paul and Barnabas.*

> *Acts 13:2-3 (NIV) 2 While they were worshiping the Lord and fasting, the Holy Spirit said, "Set apart for me Barnabas and Saul for the work to which I have called them." 3 So after they had fasted and prayed, they placed their hands on them and sent them off.*

I believe that the Lord has a purpose for each one of our lives. As we avail ourselves in His Presence, I believe that He will speak to us and reveal His Vision for our lives.

What does a vision look like?

A Vision consists of many parts.

A Vision could reveal an assignment

A vision could reveal *an <u>assignment</u>, something you should go and do* or accomplish. This was *the case* for *Abraham,* and the Apostle's *Peter and Paul.*

- *Abraham* was called out of his Father's land, to go to a country he has never been to before.
- *Peter* was *sent to go to Cornelius' house* to share the Gospel to them.
- *Cornelius* was called, through an Angelic Vision, *to send someone* to go and *find Peter*, and to bring him to them with a message.
- *Paul* was *sent to Macedonia* through a vision.

In *these visions*, we *see* that *a place, a name*, and *a purpose,* was *clearly defined.* Many times, this is the same, when God gives us an *open vision, revealing His plans* and *purposes.*

A Vision could reveal a situation

A vision could be *a revelation of a present, past or future situation* in *a nation, city, family,* or *someone's life.*

The *vision might reveal actual happenings, potential danger or warnings.* The vision might also reveal what God has in store for individuals or groups of people.

Abraham had such visions. This was the case when *the Angels visited Abraham,* en route *to destroy Sodom* and *Gomorrah. God revealed the sinful state* of the *cities*, and what the Angels were assigned to do.

There was *no instruction to Abraham* about that *terrible situation*, except that *we know* that *Abraham pleaded with God* to save the cities. *Lot also had an Angelic visit, with a message*, regarding *the same situation*. The *same Angels went to Lot* with a *clear message* to "*get out of the city*," and to "*not look back.*"

Most of the *Prophets* had *open visions*, or *angelic encounters*, through which it *was revealed*, How *God saw* the *depraved situation* of *His people*, and *what He planned to do*, *unless they turned* from *their ways.*

Visions also calls for self-initiated action

These kind of visions, brings *revelations*, which *calls for action* on *our part, especially to foil* the *plans* of the *enemy*. This was the case with Elijah, Elisha, and in the life of Jesus and His Disciples.

Elisha had these kind of visions

Elisha had these visions from God, where God showed him the plans and strategies of the enemy. Elisha, acted on these visions, by informing, and forewarning the Kings of Israel. His actions spared the Israelites many battles.

> 2 Kings 6:8-12 (NIV) 8 *Now the king of Aram was at war with Israel. After conferring with his officers, he said, "I will set up my camp in such and such a place." 9 **The man of God sent word to the king of Israel:** "Beware of passing that place, because the Arameans are going down there." 10 So the king of Israel checked on the place indicated by the man of God. **Time and again Elisha warned the king, so that he was on his guard in such places.** 11 This enraged the king of Aram. He summoned his officers and demanded of them, "**Tell me! Which of us is on the side of the king of Israel?**" 12 "**None of us, my lord the king,**"*

said one of his officers, "but Elisha, the prophet who is in Israel, tells the king of Israel the very words you speak in your bedroom."

Jesus foresaw a vision of Satan's scheme

Jesus had a vision of Satan requesting the Father that he might sift the disciples. Jesus' response to that vision was that He prayed and interceded for the disciples.

> *Luke 22:31-32 (NIV) 31 "Simon, Simon, Satan has asked to sift all of you as wheat. 32 **But I have prayed for you**, Simon, **that your faith may not fail.** And when you have turned back, strengthen your brothers."*

This action of Jesus thwarted the scheme of the enemy.

In Closing

God has a plan for your life. Find out what it is and fulfil it. Follow the dream God has for your life. ***Fulfill His purpose.***

The next area, we will look at developing, and encouraging, within our disciples, is to set ***Godly Goal.***

Action Steps

What do we need to do when we receive a vision?

1. Write down the vision.

The Lord told *Habakkuk* to write down the vision.

> *Habakkuk 2:2-3 (NIV) 2 Then the LORD replied: "**Write down the revelation and make it plain on tablets** so that a herald may run with it. 3 For the revelation awaits an appointed time; it speaks of the end and will not prove false. Though it lingers, wait for it; it will certainly come and will not delay."*

The Lord told *Jeremiah* to **write down the Words** God spoke to him.

> *Jeremiah 30:2 (NIV) 2 "This is what **the LORD**, the God of Israel, says: 'Write in a book all the words** I have spoken to you."*

> *Jeremiah 36:2 (NIV) 2 "**Take a scroll and write on it all the words I have spoken to you** concerning Israel, Judah and all the other nations from the time I began speaking to you in the reign of Josiah till now."*

The Lord told **Moses and Isaiah** to **write down the words** and messages God spoke to them.

> *Exodus 17:14 (NIV) 14 Then the LORD said to Moses, "**Write this on a scroll** as something to be remembered and make sure that Joshua hears it, because I will completely blot out the name of Amalek from under heaven."*

> *Isaiah 30:8 (NIV) 8 Go now, **write it on a tablet** for them, **inscribe it on a scroll**, that for the days to come it may be an everlasting witness.*

We also see this *practice continued* in the *New Testament*. Unless the Apostles wrote down the words and actions of the Lord Jesus, we would not have the Gospels.

> *Revelation 1:19 (NIV) 19 "Write, therefore, **what you have seen**, what is now and what will take place later."*

It is a good practice to *keep a journal* of everything God speaks to you about. Keeping record of the Words of the Lord, since they serve multiple purposes.

- *Firstly*, it serves as a constant *reminder* that *God did speak*, and
- *Secondly*, it *reminds us* of the *exact message* He spoke, and
- *Thirdly*, it serves as *placeholder* in our lives, where we can *hold on to the Promises* God gave us. The placeholder allows us to wait with expectation, and as a place where we can constantly *remind God, of His promises* to us.

In a few words, write down the personal promises God gave you already, either by revelation, prophetic Word, Scripture, or through someone else. _____

_____

_____

_____

_____

_____

2. Rewrite the Vision for everyone to understand.

In *most cases,* it seems that *the bigger the vision, the more people are impacted,* and *involved* with the *fulfilment, of the Vision. Since* many *people* will be *involved* in seeing the vision, God gave you, fulfilled, *you need to write it down in a way* that those who will *form part of it might* see and *understand their part* in fulfilling that Vision.

Habakkuk 2:2 (NIV) The LORD's Answer 2 Then the LORD
   *replied: "**Write down the revelation** and **make it plain** on*
   tablets so that a herald may run with it.

Take a moment now and write down the vision in an even more simplified way. Make it plain, so that everyone, who will form part of it, may understand, their part in it. _____

_____
_____
_____
_____
_____
_____
_____
_____
_____

Take a moment to identify the amount of people you will need alongside you to fulfill that vision. Also outline their role, function and involvement. _____

_____
_____
_____
_____
_____
_____

3. Act on the vision.

The *first way,* in which we *act on a vision,* is by *writing it down. Once* you've *written it plainly,* for *others to understand,* then you need to *make it known,* to the *extent,* to which God would want *others* to be *involved, or* for as much as *others* might be *affected,* or *impacted,* by the *message.*

   Paul and his companions *acted immediately on the vision* God gave Paul during the night.

*Acts 16:9-10 (NIV) 9 During the night **Paul had a vision** of a man of Macedonia standing and begging him, "Come over to Macedonia and help us." 10 **After Paul had seen the vision,** we **got ready at once to leave for Macedonia,** concluding that God had called us to preach the gospel to them.*

Take a moment and describe how you will make the vision known. Describe the actions steps you will take to share with others what God called you to do, and How they could become involved. __

3

SET GODLY GOALS

Goals *are important* to *everyone* who *wants to go forward* and advance to a bigger and *better place in life. How we set goals* is *as important* as *having goals*. For us as Believers, and more specifically, *as Christian Leaders*, we *set goals in accordance* with the *revealed Will of God*, as well as, according to the *Prophetic words* of the Lord to us, and for His people. We *keep* the *Promises of God alive* in your hearts, by the way we *focus* on *our goals, daily.*

> *Jeremiah 29:11 For I know the plans I have for you," declares the LORD, "plans to prosper you and not to harm you, plans to give you hope and a future.*

This Scripture is important to us, since *it declares how important planning is to God.* God has plans for us. God's plan for our lives is good. *He plans to prosper us* and to do good things for us. What that means is that *God set a goal,* of *what He plans,* to *see accomplished* in our lives. In the end, He wants to see that we prospered in accordance with His plan. *The goals He set, will be reached.*

The KJV actually says: *"to give you an expected end."*

"Without a goal, there can be no expected end."

Godly Goals, *determine* the *expected ends*, we hope for.

1. Start with what God revealed, *to all of us,* **already.**

The first step is to *start* with the <u>*generally known Purpose,*</u> that we believe, *God placed before each one* of us, such as *fulfilling the Great* <u>*Commission,*</u> as described in both Matthew chapter 28 and Mark chapter 16.

> *Matthew 28:19-20 (NIV) 19 "Therefore go and **make disciples** of all nations, **baptizing them** in the name of the Father and of the Son and of the Holy Spirit, 20 and **teaching them to obey** everything I have commanded you. And surely, I am with you always, to the very end of the age."*

> *Mark 16:15 (NIV) 15 He said to them, "Go into **all the world** and **preach the gospel** to all creation.*

Our common goal is to *"go,"* and *"preach the gospel,"* and *"baptise"* the Believers, and *"disciple them"* by *"teaching them to obey everything"* *Jesus taught us.* In our heart of hearts, we have this *desire* to *see people come to know Christ as Lord,* but then *also* to *see* those, who *respond affirmatively,* to our Gospel message, *baptised and discipled.*

Now, even though this is the general purpose, or vision, to fulfil for every believer, *each of us have a more specific part to play* in *fulfilling* the *Great Commission.* By first determining the general Vision, it then helps us keep the specific vision, we believe God placed before us, sheltered from being railroaded by outside interferences. The ultimate goal should see this general purposed fulfilled, even though it might just be in part.

2. Start with what you are passionate about.

The **second step** to take, in *setting up goals,* is to *determine the specific area,* where you believe, God would have you *serve, specifically.* This specific area of service will also see the general purpose of God fulfilled. We often see that the things we are naturally passionate about, and things He asks us to do, aligned.

During one of the *Weekend encounters* in *Step 3*, we determined our *spiritual gifts. Now* is *a good time* to *seek* for *an opportunity* to *fulfill that purpose* of God on your life.

Maybe you are *a teacher,* or *exhorter,* then now is a good time to *make yourself available* to the Leaders, to *assist* in *Teaching others,* as part of *fulfilling the Great Commission.* You could be *part of the equipping team* who *teach* the *Weekend encounter courses,* or maybe God is calling you to *equip* those whom you led to salvation, in the *confines of a small group* at home. *Whichever* of these two *excites you most,* and *at the same time scares you,* is *possibly the area where the Lord* would *have you serve* now.

Maybe you learnt that *God anointed you* to be an *Evangelist,* then now is a *good time* to put the *skills you picked up* during the *Faith Sharing Weekend* encounter into *practice. Depending on* where you are at in your Faith-walk with God, it might *start off* by *sharing your faith* with your *immediate family* and *close friends,* since the thought of *sharing with strangers scares you* too much, *or* you might venture out to do *street evangelism,* or even *open-air crusades.*

The *main point* is this: *determine the specific area, in which you believe, you can best fulfill the vision God gave you.* Sometimes this requires us to explore unfamiliar territory. Know this that God called and designed you for this purpose long ago already, and *He promised to not leave* or *forsake you* when you venture out to fulfill His great purpose for your life.

It is not uncommon for people to be uncertain about what they believe God's Vision for their lives is.

3. Start with what *others affirm* over your life.

A *Third place to start* is to *check in with friends,* for what *they believe* to be *God's purpose for you. Your Pastor*, or *the one who is discipling you* at the moment, might be *good people to check in with*, in *setting goals to fulfil*, God's great purpose.

Sometimes *the answer is right* there *in front of us,* and *we can't see* it, *yet*, when *others point it out* to us, *we find* a sense of *peace and certainty. Submit* the specific, godly assigned area *to prayer*. I often find that the *Holy Spirit will confirm* and affirm the assignment as well as give me an overwhelming sense of peace that I am on the *right track* and moving in the *right direction.*

Once you get excited about expanding God's Kingdom by doing what you believe God anointed you for, then *write down exactly what you believe He wants you to do.*

4. *Determine* your goals.

I once heard someone say that *you consume an elephant one bite at a time.* I believe that, *if we* want to see the vision, God gave us, fulfilled, then we need to *reduce the vision* into *smaller*, more *attainable steps.*

The Bible teaches us this principle in Habakkuk:

> Habakkuk 2:2 (NIV) The LORD's Answer 2 Then the LORD
> replied: "*Write down the revelation* and *make it plain on tablets* so that a herald may *run with it.*

One way of making the goals attainable, is by setting achievable goals. For instance:

- **I will share the Gospel with One person this week.**

If you do just this one little thing, then at the end of one year you will have shared the gospel with 52 people.

- **3/20 Rule of Thumb**

The marketing *rule of thumb* applies aptly here: It determines that for *every twenty people you approach*, and *share* the *Gospel*, at worst, *three people will respond* to the *presentation*.

If that be *true in* the *marketing* world, *how much more effective* will *we be*, with the *help of the Holy Spirit's conviction*, the *power in the gospel* message, and *the Lord working with us* to *confirm His Word*? *While* we *speak*, the *Holy Spirit works* on the *inside* of a person, to *bring conviction* of sin, the *Word is activated*, and the *Lord brings them* to a *place of responsiveness* where *faith rises,* to *believe the message,* and they are *born again. All of this because you set a goal* of *sharing the gospel once a week.*

Is once a week realistic?

Of course, it *is realistic*, for the average Believer who live and work around other people. By *breaking down the vision* of *"preaching the Good news"* to the whole world, into *smaller achievable goals* we will be *able to fulfill the Vision* God gave each of us.

No one starts by having *a church of 1000 people*, no, you *start* by *reaching a few worthy people first*, who in turn will disciple other worthy people who will also be able to teach others. *On this trajectory,* we *finally see* our *vision fulfilled.*

- *Set small goals that are within your faith reach.*

These are *goals*, that you, *will be able to reach*, with the *Help* of the *Holy Spirit.*

Take time over the *next two weeks*, to *set attainable goals*, to *fulfill the vision, God gave you. Once* you *determined* these *goals, share them* with *your Discipler,* and *closest friends. They* will be *better placed* to *know* whether *these are achievable, faith-filled goals*, for you to achieve.

Most godly goal setting scares me, as it *seems impossible*, yet when I *stick to* the *daily commitment,* to do what is *before me,* with diligence, I *always find myself looking back,* over my life, with *gratitude and amazement*, for the Grace of God, to see the *impossible becoming possible.*

Conclusion

Another area we keep in the forefront of our disciple's lives is to continue, year after year, to *build wider rings*, like on a tree, *values for which we will be known.* We call it the *character development* focus.

Action Steps

1. Determine your part in fulfilling the Great Commission, by defining the top three things you believe God called you to be engaged in.

I believe, God called me to _____

_____

_____

_____

_____

_____

_____

2. Complete the statement. *I believe that God anointed me to* _____

_____

_____

_____

_____

_____

_____

3. What, bite-size, steps will you take to fulfill God's Call and Anointing on your life? Name at least two action steps you will start with, and be held accountable to, to fulfilling these godly goals? ____

_____

_____

_____

_____

_____

_____

_____

_____

4. What do you expect to be recorded in Heaven about God's plan for your life? _____

_____

_____

_____

CHARACTER DEVELOPMENT

To *be characterised* as *a loving* person, a *kind* person, a *patient* person, or characterised for any of the Kingdom values, *we are required* to be *intentional about developing* those *values* into our lives. *Value*s are *determined by what, and Who, we value* most. A *commitment* to *character development*, is a *commitment to know*, and *be, like Jesus.*

We want to be like Christ

As *followers of Christ*, we *show How much* we *value Him*, and all He represents to us, that we, essentially, *want to be like Him. If we value,* for instance, *His Faithfulness*, then we will *pursue ways* to *be Faithful. If we want* to be *characterised* as *a faithful* person, *like Jesus*, then *we need* to *embrace, being Faithful,* with all of our hearts. It is *not an optional concept* to *embrace* or *not to embrace*. It becomes a *requirement for us,* but more than it being a requirement, as a *pure expression of our love* and *appreciation* of Him, *we want to live the way He wants* us to live.

The *extent* to which *we value* and *appraise Christ* in our lives, is the *extent* to which *we will pursue ways,* to *build,* into our lives, *character-istics* that *resemble Him.*

The Apostle Paul expressed this desire: *"to know Christ,"* and to *"becoming like Him." The more* we *closely walk* and *"know"* someone, the more *we become like them.*

> Philippians 3:10 (NIV) 10 *I want to know Christ*—yes, to know the power of his resurrection and participation in his sufferings, *becoming like him* in his death,

Paul warns Titus that *some deny Christ by* their *actions,* by the *values* they put *on display.* He defines those *"actions,"* as *bad character-istics.* These people were characterised, by *acting* with *opposing values,* as what their *confession demanded.*

> Titus 1:16 (NIV)
> 16 They claim to know God, but by *their actions they deny him.* They are detestable, disobedient and unfit for doing anything good.

The Apostle John declared it, quite simply, that we show that we have come to know Christ by our obedience to follow His instructions and by living like He did. *Character development* is nothing different from *pursuing to live,* and *to be, like Jesus.*

> 1 John 2:3 (NIV) 3 We know that *we* have *come to know him* if *we keep* his *commands.*

> 1 John 2:6 (NIV) 6 Whoever claims to live in him *must live as Jesus did.*

Paul addresses this, *character development,* with his spiritual son, Timothy.

Timothy

The Apostle Paul instructed Timothy to "*train*" himself "*to be godly.*"

> *1 Timothy 4:7 (NIV) 7 Have nothing to do with godless myths and old wives' tales; rather, **train yourself to be godly.***

Ruth

Boaz commended *Ruth* for her *noble character.*

> *Ruth 3:10-11 (NIV) 10 "The LORD bless you, my daughter," he replied. "This kindness is greater than that which you showed earlier: You have not run after the younger men, whether rich or poor. 11 And now, my daughter, don't be afraid. I will do for you all you ask. **All the people** of my town **know** that **you are a woman of noble character.**"*

The Bible actually tells us that: "*all the people of the town*" **knew her to be** "*a woman of noble character.*" What an **amazing testimony** that a **whole town know you to be** a person of **noble character.**

Berean Brethren

In the New Testament we read about **the Berean Believers** who were regarded for their **nobility in character.**

> *Acts 17:11 (NIV) 11 Now the **Berean** Jews **were of more noble character** than those in Thessalonica, for they received the message with great eagerness and examined the Scriptures every day to see if what Paul said was true.*

The **noble character** of these **Berean Brethren** inspired **many** throughout the ages to **follow in their footsteps.**

How do we develop this?

There seem to be *a pathway of developing* a *godly character*, and ultimately hope in our lives. The writer of Romans outlines this process in Chapter 5.

> *Romans 5:3-4 (NIV) 3 Not only so, but we also glory in our sufferings, because we know that **suffering produces perseverance;** 4 **perseverance, character;** and **character, hope.***

The Apostle Peter, in his second pastoral letter exhorts Believers to "***make every effort to add to their faith**,*" and then go on to name a number of *Kingdom Values* to add.

> *2 Peter 1:5-8 (NIV) 5 For this very reason, **make every effort** to **add to your faith goodness;** and to goodness, **knowledge;** 6 and to knowledge, **self-control;** and to self-control, **perseverance;** and to perseverance, **godliness;** 7 and to godliness, **mutual affection;** and to mutual affection, **love.** 8 For **if you possess** these **qualities in increasing measure, they will keep you from** being **ineffective,** and **unproductive,** in your knowledge of our Lord Jesus Christ.*

Peter encourages us that if we "***possess these***" characteristics "***in increasing measure***" that they will both ***keep us from*** being "***ineffective and unproductive***" as well as more, "knowledgeable" of our Lord Jesus.

I pray that each one of you will take the pathway of intentionally adding to your faith godly values and characteristics.

Action Steps

How do we do this?

1. Consider how you desire to best represent the Kingdom of God? Jot down the top seven characteristics you desire to be known by.

_____

_____

_____

_____

_____

_____

_____

2. Study these predetermined characteristics, and jot down, one or more, key Scriptures, which compelled you in your pursuit, of having these characteristics instilled in your life.

_____

_____

_____

_____

_____

_____

_____

3. Devote the next 7 days to assimilate, and install, each of these in your character, and then revise them weekly for about seven weeks. After the initial seven weeks, revisit each individual characteristic, over a three-day period, for assimilation. Once this second round of twenty-one-days period is over, repeat the process over a final seven-day period.

Coordinate this process *with* both an *accountability partner* as well as your *Discipler*. The accountability partner *could be a spouse* or some *other Believer* who *spend* a significant amount of *recreational or occupational time* with you. The *purpose is* to have someone *walk alongside you to encourage you* during your pursuit to "*add to your faith*" predetermined characteristics.

Remember that ***this is for your own development***. It is ***not a competition*** where we compare ourselves with the progress of others, but ***rather a pursuit*** to ***please the One*** in whose ***footsteps we follow***. This is that intentional process of ***making His Name known***, Becoming ***known as*** a ***Christian***.

> *Acts 11:25-26 (NIV) 25 Then Barnabas went to Tarsus to look for Saul, 26 and when he found him, he brought him to Antioch. So, for a whole year Barnabas and Saul met with the church and taught great numbers of people.* ***The disciples were called Christians first at Antioch.***

Another area we intentionally and prayerfully develop within our disciples relates to their gifting and calling. In the fourth place we focus on Gift development.

5

GIFT DEVELOPMENT

The Apostle *Paul frequently encouraged* the Believers to *"eagerly desire spiritual gifts,"* especially *those* that *build up the church.*

*1 Corinthians 12:31 (NIV) 31 Now **eagerly desire** the greater gifts.*

*1 Corinthians 14:1 (NIV) 1 Follow the way of love and **eagerly desire gifts of the Spirit**, especially **prophecy.***

One of the *greatest gifts* and *blessings we* as Believers *have received* is *the Gift of the Holy Spirit. Through* the *Holy Spirit's empowerment, we* can *receive Gifts* that no one else has or can use. *One* of the *blessings* of the *Gifts of the Holy Spirit* is that through *their use* the *Church is built up, encouraged, empowered*, and people's *lives* richly *impacted.*

1 Corinthians 12:11 (NIV) 11 All these are the work of one and the same Spirit, and he distributes them to each one, just as he determines.

The *Gifts does not cost* us anything, we *receive the Gifts* by the

Grace bestowed upon us, *just as the Holy Spirit determines*, however, *we need* to *eagerly desire* them.

How do we receive these Gifts?

Desire

A good *departure point*, in receiving these Spiritual Gifts, is to *determine which Gifts you desire,* to be *used in, by the Holy Spirit*, and *then set your affections* on *them.* Apostle *Paul* strongly *advocates this point,* in his pastoral letter to the Church in Corinth, when *he directed* their *attention,* to *especially desire, the Gift of Prophecy,* since the *church receives encouragement*, and *strengthening*, through its use.

> *1 Corinthians 14:1-3 (NIV) 1 Follow the way of love and eagerly desire gifts of the Spirit, especially prophecy. 2 For anyone who speaks in a tongue does not speak to people but to God. Indeed, no one understands them; they utter mysteries by the Spirit. 3 But the one who prophesies speaks to people for their strengthening, encouraging and comfort.*

Impartation

A *second way* in which *we receive* and *develop spiritual Gifts* in *our lives*, and *that of our Disciples*, is *by impartation*. We, *as Disciplers, play a key role* in the *growth and development* of *our disciples*.

We *constantly pray over* those *entrusted* to *our care*, not just for *their wellbeing* but *also* for *their growth* and *developmental progress*. As *we pray, we ask* the Lord, as to *the Gifts He desires* me *to impart*, and *activate*, in their lives. This is *the pattern* we *learn* from the *way Paul discipled*, and *imparted spiritual Gifts*, to *Timothy*.

> *Romans 1:11 (NIV) 11 For I am yearning to see you, that I may impart and share with you some spiritual gift to strengthen and establish you;*

> *2 Timothy 1:6 (NIV) 6 For this reason I remind you to **fan into***
> ***flame the gift of God**, which is **in you through the laying on of***
> ***my hands**.*

Activation

A *third way we* can *grow and develop, spiritual Gifts*, in our disciples, is *by activating them*. As leaders, *we* constantly *pray over our disciples*, to *learn what gifts*, the *Holy Spirit, desires to activate*. *After receiving revelation of* the *Gifts* of God *on a disciple, we Activate it,* by *declaring it* over their lives, and through the *laying on of hands,* and by constantly, *fanning it into flame.*

Encourage living, in the fullness of the Holy Spirit

Another way of *growing and developing the Gifts* of the Holy Spirit *in our lives*, is by *living in* the *Fullness of the Holy Spirit*. I often think about, *what it means,* when the *Bible speaks* about someone, being "*full of the Holy Spirit.*"

The *Bible speaks* about this *Believer* in the *Church in Jerusalem*. It was *recorded*, that *Stephen* was a man, "*Full of faith, and of the Holy Spirit.*" He most *certainly demonstrated something,* that would *attract such commendation*. He possibly *demonstrated it* by *the gifts he operated in,* as well as by *his sensitivity* and *response to* the *Holy Spirit*.

> *Acts 6:5 (NIV) 5 This proposal pleased the whole group. They chose*
> *Stephen, a man **full of faith and of the Holy Spirit**; ...*

It is *clear,* that he was "*full of the Holy Spirit,*" *while* he was *stoned* to death. The *Bible says* that, *he kept on testifying,* as well as *practice* the *courage,* to "*forgive those, who was busy stoning* him, and *ask God to forgive* them." This was a *clear demonstration* of *someone, under* the *influence,* of the *Holy Spirit*.

. . .

Another Disciple who was **known** to be *"full of the Holy Spirit,"* who later became an Apostle, is **Barnabas.** He was the **main Discipler of Paul,** and one who *saw many come to the Lord,* through his life and ministry. *Acts chapter 11 tells* us of *his reputation* and *Kingdom advancing influence.*

> *Acts 11:24 (NIV) 24 **He was** a good man, **full of the Holy Spirit and faith,** and a great number of people were brought to the Lord.*

What will it take to have such a reputation?

I believe that *an intentional pursuit to be used by the Holy Spirit,* in *all the Gifts* of the Spirit, *will* most certainly *advance us,* towards *a greater walk,* in the *fullness* of the *Holy Spirit.* The *accompanying, Fruit of the Spirit,* are *tell-tale signs,* of *a walk in the Spirit. We pursue* this, *Fullness* of the *Holy Spirit,* since *we desire,* to *be instruments* in the *Hand of God,* to *bring change* and *transformation,* in the *lives of people,* for the *Glory of God.*

Action Steps

What are the next steps to take?

- **Prayerfully make a list of the top 7 Gifts and Fruit, you desire.**

Make a list of the *seven Gifts,* you most desire, to have in your life.

_____

_____

_____

_____

_____

_____

_____

Now, also make a list, of the seven Fruit of the Spirit, you most desire, to see become part of who you are.

_____

_____

_____

_____

_____

_____

_____

Once you determined your list, then pair these Gifts and Fruit for meditation and assimilation into your life.

_____

_____

_____

_____

_____

_____

_____

- **Study these Gifts and Fruit.**

Take a two-week journey of study, in preparation, and prior, to undertaking the 7-3-1 journey, with each of these, paired, Gifts and Fruit.

Journal the specific, insights, you are learning, from the Holy Spirit, each day.

_____

_____

_____

_____

_____

_____

_____

_____

_____

_____

_____

_____

_____

_____

_____

_____

_____

_____

_____

_____

_____

_____

_____

_____

_____

_____

_____

_____

_____

_____

- **Take the 7-day, 3-day, and 1-day journey of assimilation.**

Devote 7 days to *pray over* each of these desired *Gifts and Fruit*, and after the initial seven weeks, revisit each one, over a three-day period, for assimilation and activation. Once this twenty-one-day period is over, repeat the process, over a seven-day period, by devoting one day per desired Gift and Fruit.

Journal, and record, those areas you wish to, explore more, or check in about, with your accountability partner, during your follow-up meetings.

_____
_____
_____
_____
_____
_____
_____
_____
_____
_____
_____
_____
_____
_____
_____
_____
_____
_____
_____
_____
_____

- **Remember your Accountability Partner**

Coordinate this process with, both an accountability partner, as well as your Discipler. The accountability partner could be a spouse, or some other Believer, as long as it is someone with whom you spend, a significant amount of recreational, or occupational time, together. The purpose is, to have someone walk alongside you, and to encourage you, during your pursuit, to "walk in the Fullness of the Holy Spirit," as well as, observing, as you step out, to flow and operate, in the various desired Gifts. In a sense it is to have someone "fan into flame" the Gifts and Fruit of the Spirit, in your life. Affirmation reinforces these Gifts and Fruit, especially when others affirm their observation, and operation in our lives.

- **Be transformed!**

I pray that each one of us will carry, this same reputation, as someone who is full of the holy Spirit, when others observe, our sensitivity, to the move of the Holy Spirit, as well as, see the Fruit of the Spirit, present in ours.

We also ensure, through our constant fellowship with our own disciples, that they remain focused, on being fruitful.

6

FRUITFULNESS

Fruitfulness is the *result* of *a combination* of *winning souls and discipling. Fruitfulness* is the *result of discipling*, our disciples, into *being obedient followers* of Jesus, *yet* at the *same time, fruitfulness is the overflow*, from a *deeply connected, relationship* with *Jesus.*

> John 15:5 (NIV) 5 *"I am the vine; you are the branches. If you remain in me and I in you, you will bear much fruit;* apart from me you can do nothing.

This relationship with *Jesus, activates in us* a *fruitfulness,* that *no human effort*, on itself, *can produce.* The more *time we spend* with *Jesus,* the more we *find ourselves* at the *right place* to meet the *right people* at the *right time.* As a *result of* this *deep relationship* with Jesus, we *more frequently* find *ourselves,* in *advantageous situations,* where we are *able,* to *share our Faith* in Jesus, *effectively.*

During *this session,* we *focus* our attention to, *the kind* of *fruitfulness,* that *will expand* and advance, *the Kingdom* of God.

- The first area is Soul-winning.

Soul-Winning

Our disciples should, by this stage in their *Discipleship journey*, *begin reproducing*, by *leading people* to *Christ*. *God wants* us to *be fruitful* and *multiply*. *The Blessing*, God *declared over* the life of *Abraham*, *centres* around, *fruitfulness* and *multiplication*.

> *Genesis 17:6 (NIV) 6 I will make you very fruitful; I will make nations of you, and kings will come from you.*

What *is clear* from this account of the "*Blessing of Abraham*," is that *it is the Lord* who *makes us fruitful. He made Jacob fruitful,* by giving him 12 sons, through whom He would later establish the twelve tribes of Israel. This was *the extended blessing of Abraham* spoken out *over Jacob's life.* Genesis chapter 28 shares this blessing declaration.

> *Genesis 28:3-4 (NIV) 3 May God Almighty bless you and make you fruitful and increase your numbers until you become a community of peoples. 4 May he give you and your descendants the blessing given to Abraham, so that you may take possession of the land where you now reside as a foreigner, the land God gave to Abraham."*

We *know now*, from the Word of God, that *it has always been God's intention,* to *include, every Believer*, in this "*blessing of Abraham.*" Let us take a quick look at what the *Word of God teaches us* about *our inclusion* and claim on this *Abrahamic Blessing*.

> *Galatians 3:7 (NIV) 7 Understand, then, that those who have faith are children of Abraham.*

This *Scripture affirms,* that *we*, who have *faith in Jesus*, are "*children of Abraham.*" Paul continues with his explanation on our inclusion of the Blessing of Abraham in verses 9 and 14.

> *Galatians 3:9 (NIV) 9 So those who **rely on faith are blessed along with Abraham,** the man of faith.*
>
> *Galatians 3:14 (NIV) 14 **He redeemed us** in order that the **blessing** given to **Abraham** might come to the Gentiles through Christ Jesus, so that **by faith we might receive** the promise of the Spirit.*

So, now we clearly see, that *it's always been God's desire,* to *include us,* with the *same blessing,* to *make us fruitful,* and to *multiply us* greatly. *I pray,* that we will carry, at the *forefront* of *our minds,* the *consciousness* of living, and walking, in *the Blessing of Abraham.*

How do we do this?

Win souls at all cost.

A late *friend of mine,* always *impressed on us,* to "*win souls at all cost.*" *Whatever it costs you* to *win a soul,* it *doesn't matter* about the cost, *as long as* you *win that soul.* All that *matters,* is that *we win souls,* as often as what *we are able. Two Scriptures,* that always *keeps me motivated,* comes from *Proverbs,* chapter 11, and *Daniel,* chapter 12.

> *Proverbs 11:30 (NIV) 30 **The fruit of the righteous** is a tree of life, and he who wins souls is wise.*
>
> *Daniel 12:3 (NIV) 3 **Those who are wise** will shine like the brightness of the heavens, and **those who lead many to righteousness, like the stars** for ever and ever.*

Nothing tells of *our fruitfulness,* as much as, the number of *souls we reach.* It's *all about* being *fruitful.* The *only fruit* that will *last, is souls.*

The *one thing* that both *tell of the depth* of *our following as a disciple* of *the Lord,* and of *our intentional pursuit* to *bring Glory* to our *Father* in Heaven, is *bearing* lasting *fruit.*

*John 15:8 (NIV) 8 This is to my Father's glory, that you bear much fruit,
showing yourselves to be my disciples.*

*John 15:16 (NIV) 16 You did not choose me, but I chose you and
appointed you so that you might go and bear fruit —fruit that will last
—and so that whatever you ask in my name the Father will give you.*

It is **through** the **discipling** of **the fruit** that **they become lasting fruit.**

- **The second area is Discipleship**

Disciple

A **commitment,** to **leading people** to **Christ, should** be **followed**
through, with **a commitment to disciple** them, in the **teachings of Jesus.**
It is **never one, or the other**, it is **always a commitment to both.** The **two
main Scriptures,** upon which we **primarily base** the **Great Commission,**
are **Matthew chapter 28,** verses 19 to 20, and then also **Mark chapter 16,**
verses 15 to 20.

*Matthew 28:19-20 (NIV) 19 Therefore go and make disciples of all
nations, baptizing them in the name of the Father and of the Son and of
the Holy Spirit, 20 and teaching them to obey everything I have
commanded you. And surely, I am with you always, to the very end of the
age."*

It might be good to remind ourselves about the **main aspects** of
this portion:

1. **"Go"** – A commitment to the Great Commission starts with a
willingness, to go, **"to all nations;"**

2. **"Make Disciples"** – A commitment to the Great Commission
requires us a commitment to **"make disciples."**

3. **"Baptise them"** – A commitment to the Great Commission
means that we are committed to see that those who accepted Christ,
also get baptised as a public testimony of their profession of faith in
the Lord Jesus; and

4. "*Teaching them to obey everything*" is a commitment to teach our disciples "everything Jesus commanded us." The fifth take away from this account of the Great Commission is that

5. "*And surely I am with you always.*" – We have this assurance from the Lord Himself that He will always be with us when we go out, to make disciples, and whilst baptising and teaching them His commands.

The *other account* of the *Great Commission* echoes the sentiments, of the Gospel of Matthew.

> *Mark 16:15-16 (NIV) 15 He said to them, "Go into **all the world** and **preach the gospel** to **all creation**. 16 **Whoever believes** and is **baptized** will be saved, but whoever does not believe will be condemned.*

What this, other, account of the Great Commission, teaches us is:

6. "*Preach the gospel*" The preaching of the Gospel of Jesus, stands central, to people putting their faith in Jesus. The preaching of Jesus should be the basis upon which people come to faith.

7. "*Whoever believes*" The purpose, and expected outcome, of sharing our faith, should culminate in people putting their faith in Jesus, as their Lord. Salvation, or, too be saved, relies on people putting their faith in Jesus Christ, as Lord and Saviour.

Conclusion

May the Lord find in us Fruitful branches, bearing much, and lasting fruit to His Glory!

Action Steps

1. Who are you trusting the Lord for, to be saved, at the moment? List your top three Names, and your involvement, and activity, in their lives.

_____

_____

_____

_____

_____

_____

2. How often do you share your faith with people around you?

_____

3. When last were you able to lead people, in a prayer, to salvation?

_____

4. What are you doing, to actively engage, people, to engage them with the Gospel?

_____

_____

_____

_____

_____

_____

5. How many people, whom you personally led to Christ, are you discipling at present?

_____

_____

_____

_____

7

RELATIONSHIPS

The *relationships we keep* and cherish *will determine* the *credibility* of *our character* and *destiny*. The *relationships* we maintain, either *help us* towards, or *keep us from*, our *God-ordained destiny*.

Proverbs 13:20 (NIV) 20 **Walk with the wise and become wise**, *for a companion of fools suffers harm.*

Psalms 14:5 (NIV) 5 *But there they are, overwhelmed with dread, for* **God is present in the company of the righteous.**

As Leaders, we model to others, how essential it is to maintain the right relationships, firstly, in our own households, and then with the circle of friends we keep company.

The Bible warns us against the keeping of bad company.

1 Corinthians 15:33 (NIV) 33 Do not be misled: "**Bad company corrupts good character.**"

*1 Timothy 3:12-13 (NIV) 12 A deacon must be faithful to his wife
and must **manage his children and his household well.** 13
Those who have served well gain an excellent standing and
great assurance in their faith in Christ Jesus.*

Our relationship with God should *determine*, and *set, the parameters,* for *every other relationship*, we enter into. This *Scripture requires*
that *a Leader*, regardless of where they think they appear in seniority,
should manage their *household well. The way* in which *they manage*
their *household* should be *reflective* of *their faith.* There *should be
consistency* between their *faith* and the *household* they lead.

This *message* is *emphasised* by *Paul,* to his disciple, *Timothy,* when
he *instructed him,* about the *requirements* he need to instil, among the
leaders, in the local churches.

*1 Timothy 5:8 (NIV) 8 **Anyone** who **does not provide** for **their relatives,**
and **especially** for their **own household,** has **denied the faith** and is worse
than an unbeliever.*

Once again, we see the *direct correlation between* the *family relationships* and *one's faith. God wants us* to *provide* for *our relatives,* especially for our *own parents, children* and *grandchildren.* The *welfare* of
our *families* is *important to God.*

Family

Our families are *important to God* and should be to us as well. I once
saw a sign that said:

*"Every man who is happy at home is a successful man, even if he has
failed in everything else."*

Let your happiness rest in and *among those* whom *God entrusted to
you.* The *most important relationship, outside* your *relationship with*

God, should be with *your spouse.* Much have been written on this, however, indulge me for a moment.

The way you treat and *love your spouse* is a *direct reflection* of how *you value* and *honor God.* The Apostle *Paul wrote* to the church in *Ephesus* and *gave* them *instructions* for *Christian Households.* He embarks on this instruction by *encouraging mutual submission,* and then make the all-important connection between our *marital relationship* and *our faith* and how *they are inter-related.*

> *Ephesians 5:21 (NIV) 21 **Submit to one another** out of reverence for*
> *Christ.*

We are encouraged to *love our wives,* in the same way *as* what *the Christ loves the church.* We *reflect our faith* by the *way we love* and *treat our spouses.*

> *Ephesians 5:25-27 (NIV) 25 **Husbands, love your wives, just as***
> ***Christ loved the church** and gave himself up for her 26 to make*
> *her holy, cleansing her by the washing with water through the*
> *word, 27 and to present her to himself as a radiant church,*
> *without stain or wrinkle or any other blemish, but holy and*
> *blameless.*

Love your spouse, in *a way* that *shows, how much* you *love the Lord.*
On another note, *regarding family,* sometimes *our family refers* to *our parents, siblings, in-laws* or *related family. Treat them* with the same **grace,** that's been *offered to you.* Sadly, *when it comes to them becoming a stumbling block* in *you fulfilling your calling* and *purpose, Jesus teaches us* that we *might have to leave* their company.

> *Matthew 19:29 (NIV) 29 And **everyone who has left houses or brothers or***
> *sisters or **father** or **mother** or **wife** or **children** or **fields** for my sake will*
> *receive a **hundred times** as much and will inherit eternal life.*

On *one occasion* the Disciples *drew Jesus' attention* to the presence of *His family waiting* for *Him outside. His response* was quite *unexpected*, yet *as we become* more *intentional* about *fulfilling God's purpose* for our lives, we will *find ourselves, considering His response, not that surprising*.

> Luke 8:21 *(NIV)* 21 *He replied, "My mother and brothers are those who hear God's word and put it into practice."*

Do I advocate separation from our dear *family members? No*, but I would *rather* have you *walk in obedience, fulfilling* the *Call of God* on your life, *than keeping the company* of *those*, who *might keep you from* your *purpose*.

Children

We should also *be attentive* to the *way we treat* our *children*. We should *not embitter them* through *harsh* and *unjust treatment*. May we be the best example of How to treat children well.

> Ephesians 6:4 *(NIV)* 4 *Fathers, do not exasperate your children; instead, bring them up* in the *training* and *instruction of the Lord.*

God truly desires that we *rather equip* and *train our children* in the *ways of the Lord*.

> Deuteronomy 6:6-7 *(NIV)* 6 *These commandments* that *I give you today* are to *be on your hearts.* 7 *Impress them* on *your children. Talk about them* when you *sit at home* and *when you walk* along the road, when you *lie down* and *get up.*

When you read, this Scripture, it once again sets the parameters, of bringing them up, "*In the training, and instruction of the Lord.*"

We honour God, when we treat our children, as gifts, and blessings from God.

Friends

Other than our *family* and *relatives*, the *next set* of, most *important relationships* we have, *are our friends.* The *company* you *keep* will *determine the impact* your *walk will have* for the *advancement* of the *Gospel.* Having *the right friends* is *important* to *keeping* and *guarding oneself.*

> Proverbs 13:20 (NIV) 20 **Walk with the wise and become wise,** *for a companion of fools suffers harm.*

> Isaiah 32:8 (NIV) 8 But **the noble make noble plans,** *and by noble deeds they stand.*

Scripture teaches us here the **great value** of **keeping company with** the **wise and noble.**

- **Consider your ways and actions when you spend time with the wise.**

One of the things, we learn from the Word of God, is that when we sit with the wise, or great, that we tame our tongue, and appetite.

A temperate person will be much more tolerated, than a loud-mouthed fool. A quiet person will be equally accommodated, and even sheltered, in the conversation of the strong and powerful. It is wise to hold one's opinions for yourself until you've developed the relationship to a level where it will be appropriate to share.

Why is this important?

You only have one chance, or at most a few, to access the wise and great. If you mess it up, it is over. You will never have such a privilege among them or their friends again. Use the opportunities that you get wisely.

I've always looked at *people whom I admire* most, and then *sought for opportunities to serve them,* just to *be in their company. I found* that, one of the *most biblical ways,* to *gain entrance* into *the company of the wise and righteous* is *to serve them* in *humility.* This biblical strategy has served me well.

Bad Company

We also need to *take heed,* to *the wisdom* shared, in these *Scriptures,* that, *if you* keep *company with fools, you will suffer harm.*

> *Psalms 1:1 (NIV) 1 Blessed is the one who does not walk in step with the wicked or stand in the way that sinners take or sit in the company of mockers,*

The *Bible calls* the *one* who *does not walk according* to the *advice* of *the wicked,* or *follow the pathways* of *sinners,* or *prefer* the *company of mockers, Blessed.*

The *Amplified Bible* states it beautifully:

> *Psalms 1:1 (AMPC) 1 BLESSED (HAPPY, fortunate, prosperous, and enviable) is the man who walks and lives not in the counsel of the ungodly [following their advice, their plans and purposes], nor stands [submissive and inactive] in the path where sinners walk, nor sits down [to relax and rest] where the scornful [and the mockers] gather.*

As a Disciple of Jesus, we *revisit* the *company we keep.* We *ensure* that, *as far as* what it is *possible,* that we *build relationships* with "*righteous, god-honoring people.*" This is *one,* valuable, aspect, to living a *blessed* and *prosperous life.* The *one thing* that will *surely corrupt* our *good character,* is *bad company.*

> *1 Corinthians 15:33 (NIV) 33 Do not be misled: "Bad company corrupts good character."*

I know that it *might be* an *overstretch,* to *discuss worldly relation-*

ship, at **this point** of your **walk with God, however** it might just be, **the prompting** and **advice you need,** to **share** with **your disciples,** who **might** still **be entangled,** in **worldly relationships.**

Since **we are talking** about **multiplication,** in **Step 5** of our **Discipleship Foundation Series,** we will **be wise** to **understand, what keeps us from barrenness,** and **simultaneously, brings us** into **fruitfulness and multiplication.** The **Bible says** that, the **company** of the **godless** will **leave you barren.**

> Job 15:34-35 (NIV) 34 For **the company of the godless will be barren,** and fire will consume the tents of those who love bribes. 35 They conceive trouble and give birth to evil; their womb fashions deceit."

Company of the wise

- **What will it take for you to come into a relationship with the wise?**

Every pursuit, in building good, godly relationships, should be well considered, prior to embarking on, building those relationships.

Serving

I believe that the first way, to build these relationships, is by serving your way into them. Genuineness, and sincerity, are essentials in serving. The humility with which you serve, will bring you before great, and wise people. Serving, will also bring you in a favourable position, to get to know them better, without having to ask interrogating questions.

> Mark 9:35 (NIV) 35 Sitting down, Jesus called the Twelve and said, "Anyone who wants to be first must be the very last, and the servant of all."

Honour

Honouring, wise and influential people, will always open up a pathway, to them. The Bible teaches that we need two show proper respect and honor.

> *1 Peter 2:17 (NIV) 17 **Show proper respect to everyone**, love the family of believers, fear God, honor the emperor.*

Few people honour others, or show respect, so, when someone does show respect and honor, it immediately draws ones attention, especially when it's offered in a sincere manner, and not as some clichéd means, to gain privileged access to someone important. Your façade will wear thin, and they will see through your pretence, if you are not sincere. However, if you will maintain a sincere honouring, of those from whom you desire to learn, it will put you in good stead, to potentially, develop those great relationships.

Showing proper respect, is a great way to, initiate the building, of great, mentoring relationships.

Gifts

The giving of gifts is another biblical way, of opening the pathway for you, to initiate, and gain access, to great relationships. The Bible teaches us that the, "***giving of gifts***," brings us before, "***the Great.***"

> *Proverbs 18:16 (NIV) 16 **A gift opens the way and ushers the giver** into the presence of **the great.***

It is not the size, or expense of the gift that matters, as much as the heart, and thoughtfulness, with which it is presented. Make it personal, to the extent that, they can see, that it was not just a random thought, but a considered thought, with them in mind, and their needs. Don't make a fuss of it either.

They will always remember you for your thoughtfulness, and

consideration. If the Lord grant you favour, you will gain greater access, and opportunity. There are many classic stories, to validate this power, of coming before "the great," with gifts. I pray that God will grant you favour, to reach "the Great," in high places.

What will make my relationships, more blessed, and prosperous?

The **Bible teaches** that, "**God is present in the company of the righteous.**" **I want to be** where **God is present** and **welcomed.** A sure way to bring blessing on my relationships, is by ensuring, that we centre the relationship around Christ. Make Him the reason, why you are pursuing the relationship. Make sure that we keep our conversations, about Him, His Will, and His purpose. Make sure that we keep Him in the consciousness of our mind, when we speak or discuss things.

> *Psalms 14:5 (NIV) 5 ..., for **God is present** in the **company of the righteous.***

Jesus said that, **when** we **gather** in **His Name, He will be there with us**, in our midst. **He is a listener,** when "**those who fear the Lord,**" **gather.** The **moment we gather with** other **Believers, He becomes** our **invited guest.** If we **desire,** to **be** in **Great Company,** then **keep the company** of **those who fear** and **revere the Lord.**

> *Malachi 3:16 (NIV) 16 Then those who feared the LORD talked with each other, and the LORD listened and heard. A scroll of remembrance was written in his presence concerning those who feared the LORD and honored his name.*

- **Choose to transition your relationships into the direction you wish to grow.**

In the beginning years of becoming a Believer, you might still have many worldly relationships. Most will immediately break off the relationship, since they think it strange that you stopped your former way of living, however, some will want to remain friends. They are often the ones who are next in line to come to Christ. Let your light shine brightly among these long-time friends.

> *1 Peter 4:4 (NIV) 4 **They are surprised that you do not join them** in their reckless, wild living, and they heap abuse on you.*

However, you are going to need to build new friendships that will help and guide you in your walk with God.

- Choose prayerfully and wisely. *Relationships can make you or break you.*
- Choose people *who will be the Barnabas* in your life.
- Choose *positive and visionary people* who inspire you.
- Choose to *build relationships* with people who are *stronger in their Faith* than you.
- Choose *people who build others up.*
- Choose *people who love God* and *people* passionately.

I pray that God will give you good and wholesome relationships, both with your spouse, your family, your relatives and friend.

Action Steps

What steps do I need to take, to build the right relationships?

- **Revisit your friendship relationships.**

Make a list of your friends, and then separate the godly ones from the ungodly. I am not saying that you simply dispose of ungodly relationship. Unless you are actively engaging the ungodly, with the intentional purpose of reaching them for Christ, then separate yourself from those relationships. ***Bad company corrupts good behaviour.***

Now, jot down the top 12, current relationships, you have.

_____

_____

_____

_____

_____

_____

_____

_____

_____

_____

_____

_____

Just before we move onto the next action step, let us revisit this list of friends, to determine our real purpose and intention in keeping and maintaining them. Prayerfully consider your current relationships.

- **Consider the kind of wise people you would love to have relationships with.**

We all know acquaintances, whom we admire, and find inspiration from, to be around. Make two lists here: one for those whom you want to come close to, to reach for Christ, and one for those whom you believe would inspire you to be a better follower in Christ. Once you have these two lists drawn, take time to ask the Holy Spirit for the top three relationships you need to pursue. The one group will consist of those you wish to reach for Christ, and the other group will comprise of those you will pursue to be Discipled, by them, and to learn from them.

1. First, list those, wise, and inspirational people, whom you would love to reach for Christ.

_____

_____

_____

_____

_____

_____

_____

2. Secondly, list those, wise, and inspirational people, you would love to come close to, so that you may learn from them.

_____

_____

_____

_____

_____

_____

_____

8

THE POWER OF ENCOURAGEMENT

One of *the biggest investments* you can *ever make* in the *lives of your disciples* is *being an encourager*. The *Bible teaches* us to *encourage one another*.

1 Thessalonians 5:11 Therefore encourage one another and build each other up, just as in fact you are doing.

We all love to be *around encouraging people*. *Encouragers* are those, *who are always positive,* and *chooses* to *highlight*, the *positive aspects*, in *every situation*.

- They are often those who *recap conversations,* and situations, with the *intention* of *closing the conversation* with some *positive takeaways*.
- They are *always affirming* some *aspect in you*, whether that be *something you did, something they noticed* or *something you are wearing*, they *always* choose to *say something positive* and *affirming*.
- They *always smile* when *they greet* you.
- They *take time to enquire* after *your wellbeing*.

- They *never speak about anyone* in *a negative way behind their back.*
- They will *always turn gossip into* an *opportunity* to *say something positive* and *upbuilding,* and sometimes even call people to uphold the people in prayer.

I am sure, *you would love to be around people,* that are *Encouragers.* If you are not an encourager today, *make a decision to become one.*

Encouraged people reproduce quicker and *faster than those who need* and *seek encouragement. Take time* to *seek ways* in which *to encourage others.*

We read in the *Book of Acts* about *a disciple,* from the *church in Antioch,* whose name was *Joseph. He was such an encourager* that *the Apostles named him Barnabas.* Barnabas was *such an encourager* that he *became known* for *his encouragement.*

Acts 4:36 (NIV) 36 *Joseph, a Levite from Cyprus, whom the apostles called Barnabas (which means "son of encouragement"),*

He is the one who *looked for Saul* and *brought him* to the *church in Antioch. He* is the one who *taught him* for *two years* before *the Holy Spirit sent the two* of them out on their *first Missionary journey.*

Do you have a Barnabas in your life?
Are you a Barnabas to your Disciples?

Personal Testimony.

I know what it means to have a *"Barnabas"* in my life. *My first Barnabas* was *a Pastor,* called, *At Geldenhuys.*

- He was *my Barnabas,* in the *developing years,* of *my ministry life.*
- He was *always available,* always *ready to listen,* always

there to *lift me up,* above the *present situation,* and *give me an eagle's view* to *bring perspective.*

- He *always affirmed my calling, gifts* and *strengths.*
- He *always reminded me* of my *accomplishments.*
- He *always reminded me* of the *Prophetic words* God gave me.
- *He loved me and my wife,* through *dark and difficult times.*
- He *always inspired me,* to *be a bigger* and *better person.*

I am *eternally grateful* for *Pastor At! Through the years, I* have *applied* those *same principles,* he taught me, in *my ministry with others. I hope,* to *be known,* as *such a "son of encouragement"* to *others.*

Paul, an example of being an encourager, who saw great multiplication.

I want to *encourage you* to be *that "son of encouragement"* to *your disciples.* The Apostle Paul *practiced* this *kind of Leadership,* as *he travelled and ministered,* throughout all of his **missionary journeys.** As a *result* of *all the Encouragement* he *brought* to *the Believers, He saw more multiplication,* than *anyone else. We read,* in at least *six of his letters,* that He wrote about, encouragement.

> *Acts 20:1-2 (NIV) 1 When the uproar had ended, Paul sent for the disciples and, after encouraging them, said goodbye and set out for Macedonia. 2 He travelled through that area, speaking many words of encouragement to the people, and finally arrived in Greece,*

Our *union with Christ brings* great *encouragement.*

Philippians 2:1-2 (NIV) 1 Therefore if you have any encouragement from being united with Christ, if any comfort from his love, if any common sharing in the Spirit, if any tenderness and compassion, 2 then make my joy

complete by being like-minded, having the same love,
being one in spirit and of one mind.

"There is a direct connection between encouragement and multiplication."

After Paul's conversion, the **churches** throughout Judea, Galilee and Samaria, **found themselves** at **peace,** from being heavily persecuted. **They** were **encouraged, by his conversion,** and **multiplied.** The moment encouragement come, then multiplication come.

Acts 9:31 (NIV) 31 Then the church throughout Judea, Galilee and Samaria enjoyed a time of peace and was strengthened. Living in the fear of the Lord and encouraged by the Holy Spirit, it increased in numbers.

Encouraged people multiply.

The **Church** in **Antioch multiplied greatly.** The **Bible tells us** that "the **Hand of the Lord was with them, and a great number of people believed."** The moment **people feel,** that **they are not alone,** and that **someone is with them,** and **behind them, we see** that, **that kind of encouragement** brings **multiplication.** This is what the **church in Antioch experienced.**

Acts 11:21 (NIV) 21 The Lord's hand was with them, and a great number of people believed and turned to the Lord.

The **Apostles knew,** just so **well,** the **impact,** the **Lord working with them,** brought, that it **resulted** in **great multiplication.** This is the **promise,** and **encouragement, Jesus gave each one,** who would **go out,** and **preach the gospel.**

Matthew 28:20 (NIV) 20 and teaching them to obey everything I have commanded you. And surely, I am with you always, to the very end of the age."

The *Apostles* were *greatly encouraged,* as they *boldly went out,* to bring *testimony* of the *Resurrected Christ.* The *difference was* that *they felt encouraged,* as *the Lord worked with them,* by *confirming His word,* and *by the signs* and *wonders* that *followed.*

> *Mark 16:20 (NIV) 20 Then the disciples went out and preached everywhere, and **the Lord worked with them and confirmed his word** by the signs that accompanied it.*

This is the *same testimony,* we started with, when *we looked* at the *impact Barnabas had,* by the *Holy Spirit,* when *he went to Antioch.*

> *Acts 11:23-24 (NIV) 23 When he arrived and saw what the grace of God had done, **he was glad and encouraged them all** to remain true to the Lord with all their hearts. 24 He was a good man, full of the Holy Spirit and faith, and **a great number of people were brought to the Lord.***

When the *Lord wanted Joshua* to *take the people* into the *Promised land, He first encouraged him.* In *one short record* of this *charge, to go* and *take possession* of the *Promised land,* the *Lord repeated two phrases,* a *few times:* "*Be strong and full of courage,*" and "*I will be with you.*" As *the Lord was with Moses,* He *was with Joshua.*

> *Joshua 1:9 (NIV) 9 Have I not commanded you? **Be strong and courageous.** Do not be afraid; **do not be discouraged,** for the LORD your God will be with you wherever you go.*"

It seems from *these few Scriptures,* that *there are* a number of *ways,* in which we *find,* and *receive, encouragement. As Leaders* who *desire* to *see* our *disciples multiply, we will* be *wise* to *embrace* the *giving of encouragement.* I pray that you will truly *become a "Barnabas"* to those *entrusted* to *your care. Encourage! Be an Encourager!*

> *1 Thessalonians 5:11 Therefore **encourage one another** and **build each other up,** just as in fact you are doing.*

Action Steps

How can we encourage other?

Think of those, whom you have been praying for, over the past couple of weeks, and choose at least three of them, that you may actively encourage them, in one, or more, of the following areas:

- Assure them that you are with them.
- Always pour courage and hope into them by sharing faith-filled Scriptures with them.
- Affirm their gifting and calling.
- Affirm God's Words over their lives.
- Encourage them with words.
- Remind them of what God accomplished in and through them.
- Minister "Rhema" words into their lives.
- Encourage their families.
- Tell others how proud you are of them.

Take time, now, to write down their names, and next to it, the way in which you will encourage, and build them up, this week.

_____

_____

_____

_____

_____

_____

Just before we move on from this weeks' time together, one more thing. Keep a journal of the people you encourage, and see, over a period of time, how you can encourage them in all of these mentioned areas. **May you be a great Encourager!**

9

FINANCES

Finances play such *an integral part* of our *daily lives.* I *once heard* someone say that *Jesus spoke more* on *finances,* than on any other, *single aspect. Finances* are *important* for our *daily sustenance.*

How we work with our *personal finances,* has a *direct impact* on *how we* will *succeed,* in *life,* and in our *ministry.*

> *1 Timothy 3:5 (NIV) 5 (If anyone does not know how to manage* his own family, *how can he take care of God's church?)*

If we Handle our *personal finances well,* then it gives us *credibility* to *work,* and *lead, in* the *local church.* There is a *direct inter-relatedness* between, *how well we fare* with our *personal finances,* and *how it impacts* our *ability* to *take care* of *God's House. If we manage* our *own family's finances well,* we *will also* be *able to* take *good care* of the *Church's finances.*

> *1 Timothy 5:8 (NIV) 8 Anyone who does not provide for their relatives, and especially for their own household, has denied the faith and is worse than an unbeliever.*

The *way* in which we *use our finances* to *provide* for our *relatives,* and *especially* our *own families, validates* our *faith. If we* are *not able* to *take care* of our *own families,* then we are in a sense, *"worse than unbelievers,"* and have *denied our faith.* We *proof* that *our faith works,* by *the way we provide,* for our *own households.*

Our ability, to *take care* of our *own needs, and* are *able to give, determines how well* we *really fare.*

Example of the Apostle Paul

The *Apostle Paul* had one of the *most successful ministries* in *New Testament* times. *One of the keys* for *his success,* was *his ability* to *take care* of *his own needs,* even when that meant that he had to *"work with his own hands,"* and live in his own *"rented house."*

> *Acts 20:33-35 (NIV) 33 I have not coveted anyone's silver or gold or clothing. 34 You yourselves know that these hands of mine have supplied my own needs and the needs of my companions. 35 In everything I did, I showed you that by this kind of hard work we must help the weak, remembering the words the Lord Jesus himself said: 'It is more blessed to give than to receive.'"*

This meant that *Paul often worked* with *his own hands,* by *making tents,* in order that he could *take care* of *his own needs,* and that of *his companions.*

> *1 Thessalonians 2:9 (NIV) 9 Surely you remember, brothers and sisters, our toil and hardship; we worked night and day in order not to be a burden to anyone while we preached the gospel of God to you.*

Sometimes in ministry, to be *able to continue* with *our ministry,* we *might be required* to *take on* a *secular job,* to *enable us* to *do the work of the Lord.* If it was a *good thing* for *Paul,* then it is *most certainly good for us.*

2 Thessalonians 3:8-9 (NIV) 8 nor did we eat anyone's food without paying for it. On the contrary, we worked night and day, labouring and toiling so that we would not be a burden to any of you. 9 We did this, not because we do not have the right to such help, but in order to offer ourselves as a model for you to imitate.

Paul gave us an example to follow. **He practiced** a **profession** he **learnt along the way.** If we **look at** his **life trajectory prior** to **being Born Again,** we **see** that it was **stooped in Studying,** and **educating himself** in **Judaism,** however, possibly **because** of the **demands on him pioneering** many **churches,** and **frequently traveling** to do so, **he learnt another trade,** to **sustain and provide** for **himself,** and **his companions.**

*Acts 18:3 (NIV) 3 and because **he was a tentmaker** as they were, **he** stayed and **worked with them.***

Personal Finances

When it comes to your *Personal finances, **make a sound assessment** of your **present debt,** and **welfare. Make sure** that, as **far as is possible,** that you **don't live in debt,** and that **no debt remains outstanding.**

- *Live within* your *means.*
- *Pay your bills on time.*
- *Pay* your *personal taxes.*

*Romans 13:8 (NIV) 8 **Let no debt remain outstanding,** except the continuing debt to love one another, for whoever loves others has fulfilled the law.*

One of the **main causes** that **gives people a bad name,** is **debt.** We **often find** that, when **people speak** about **someone having a bad reputation,** that it is **often related** to their, **inability,** to **handle finances.**

*1 Timothy 3:7 (NIV) 7 He **must** also **have a good reputation** with*
outsiders, so that he will not fall into disgrace and into the devil's trap.

Ministry Finances

When *we handle* our *finances well*, it also *protects our ministry's reputa-*
tion. Handle Ministry finances with even *greater caution,* as with *your*
own, since we are simply, *just Stewards,* of *His resources,* and *will* have
to *give account,* of our *entrustment. Sometimes,* we *receive funds* for
some *events, make sure* that *you account* for it, *well. Sometimes,* we
receive *an offering,* or *donations* for *a cause, make sure* that these *funds*
are *recorded well,* and *reach* their *intended cause.*

The key word for handling ministry finances well, is the word
"*BUDGET.*" The extent to which you *prepare a budget, maintain the*
budget, and *work according to the budget,* is the extent to which you
will be *deemed a good steward* of the resources of God.

As *Leaders,* we have to *check in* with *our disciples,* about how they
are *tracking, in their finances as well. Financial strain* often *bleeds into*
behaviour, and *relationships. Before* these *attitudes* become *personal,*
check in with *your disciples,* to see *how you could walk with them,*
through *whatever,* they might be *facing.* Remember to *encourage, more*
than, giving advice, or *guidance!*

Regularly, check in on *them,* and *ensure* that they are *well cared* for.
If it *goes well* with *them,* they *will succeed,* and *fruitfulness ensured.*

Caution

Also, *remember* that the *seed was smothered,* in the *second to last phase,*
in the *Parable of the Sower,* due to the "*deceitfulness of riches.*" *Watch*
over those, *entrusted* to *your care,* that they *do not find themselves*
entangled, or *lured* into, "*Get-rich-quick-schemes,*" or into "*pyramid*
schemes," because of their *increased network* of *leaders.* Network
marketers, especially target, growing churches with networks of discipleship groups. *Be careful!* I have seen more churches destroyed

because of network businesses, that collapse, than of any other moral, or fiscal failure.

Encourage financial success and growth

Through the life of Christ, we are encouraged to break out of poverty, into a prosperous life.

> *Jeremiah 29:11 (NIV) 11 For **I know the plans I have for you,"** declares the LORD, **"plans to prosper you** and not to harm you, plans to give you hope and a future.*

> *2 Corinthians 8:9 (NIV) 9 For you know the grace of our **Lord Jesus Christ,** that **though he was rich,** yet for your sake **he became poor,** so **that you through his poverty might become rich.***

It is God's plan to prosper His Children. Through the Grace of our Lord Jesus Christ, He became poor, that we might become rich. God desires that we prosper, in every aspect of our lives.

> *3 John 1:2 (NKJV) 2 Beloved, **I pray that you may prosper in all things** and be in health, **just as your soul prospers.***

God desires that ***we prosper*** in ***every aspect*** of ***our*** lives. We ***sometimes see,*** the ***most promising disciples, not bear,*** the ***expected thirty, sixty*** or ***hundredfold harvest,*** and that, all ***because their finances*** went ***out of order.***

May we ***lead by*** our ***example,*** and ***not, to entice others,*** to ***live beyond their means. Sometimes, disciples*** want to ***please us,*** by ***showing progress,*** by ***taking social lifts, beyond*** their ***means.*** This could be, by ***unnecessarily, purchasing things*** to ***wear,*** new ***bicycles, Motorbikes, cars,*** or by ***purchasing,*** or ***building houses,*** close to ***where we live.*** Encourage people, through our example, that it is far more expedient to lay up treasures in Heaven, than on earth.

*Matthew 6:19-21 (NIV) 19 "Do not store up for yourselves treasures
on earth, where moths and vermin destroy, and where thieves
break in and steal. 20 But **store up for yourselves treasures in
heaven**, where moths and vermin do not destroy, and where
thieves do not break in and steal. 21 For **where your treasure is,
there your heart will be also.***

*Hebrews 13:5 (NIV) 5 **Keep your lives free from the love of money
and be content with what you have**, because God has said,
"**Never will I leave you; never will I forsake you.**"*

We can help our disciples by, not stressing our accomplishments, as much as, rather focus on their accomplishments and successes. May we live, content, with what we have, and who we have in our lives.

Action Steps

1. Do you have a budget? _____

2. What debts do you have? _____

_____

_____

_____

_____

_____

3. Which debts are you able to pay-off if you sell some of what you own? _____

_____

_____

4. What keeps you from living debt free? _____

_____

_____

_____

_____

5. What difference will it make on your relationships if you reduce, and even, become debt free? _____

_____

_____

_____

6. How open and transparent are you with your Mentor about your real financial status? _____

_____

7. Making a commitment to live debt free, is the first step in the right direction. What other steps will you take to bring your finances into alignment with Romans 13 verse 8? _____

_____

_____

_____

_____

_____

10

DEALING WITH SETBACKS

W henever, *anyone sets out* to *do anything for God*, they *will encounter opposition*, from the *Evil one*. *Satan* always *attempts to stop* the *advancement*, of the *Kingdom of God*. Because of *his resistance*, we often *find* ourselves *dealing*, with *many obstacles*, *however*, *we* do *not warfare* as *those* who *have no hope*.

Matthew 16:18 (NIV) 18 And I tell you that you are Peter, and on this rock, I will build my church, and the gates of Hades will not overcome it.

With these *words* in our *hearts*, *we walk* and *persevere*, since *the One* who *promised it*, *is Faithful*, and *He* who *started this good work*, in *us*, and in *our disciples*, *will continue* it until it's completed. This does *not take away* the, *sometimes challenging*, *situations we* have to *endure*. We might *at times pray* the *words* of the *Psalmist*:

Psalms 123:3-4 (NIV) 3 Have mercy on us, LORD, have mercy on us, for we have endured no end of contempt. 4 We have endured no end of ridicule from the arrogant, of contempt from the proud.

In *seeing* our *disciples grow* in *Christ*, and *ultimately be fruitful* and *multiply*, we *will encounter* many *confrontational situations. Most of it* will *have* a *positive outcome*, and *be good* for *us*, however, *this session* is *to prepare us,* for *those times,* when *things don't turn out* the *way we anticipated,* when we *embarked* on this *discipleship journey*, together.

A *few scenarios* might *confront us*, and *require our preparation*, on *how we will deal* with them, on this *Discipleship Journey*:

- *How to deal with failure?*
- *How to deal with betrayal?*
- *How to deal with rejection?*
- *How to deal with trials?*
- *How to deal with despondency?*

Discipling people is exciting, but challenging

Discipling people is *exciting* but *challenging* at the *best of times*. To see *visions fulfilled*, will *cost you*, and there *is a price to pay*, to *seeing disciples grow*, to *fulfill, God's purpose* in their *lives*. However, *the cost* of *being a Discipler* is *outweighed*, by *the eternal treasures stored up* for *those* of us who *faithfully follow*, this *dream of God*.

Jesus prepared His Disciples, for the challenges they would face

Jesus, in His *first teaching* to *His Disciples, laid* this *foundation. He equipped*, His *Disciples*, to *be prepared* for *all kinds* of *abuse, slander, evil words*, and *mistreatment. He prepared* them, with *a reminder, that, "the prophets were persecuted,* in the *same way."*

> *Matthew 5:10-12 (NIV), "Blessed are those who are persecuted because of righteousness, for theirs is the kingdom of heaven. Blessed are you when people insult you, persecute you and falsely say all kinds of evil against you because of me. Rejoice and be glad, because great is your reward in heaven, for in the same way they persecuted the prophets who were before you."*

Preparing ourselves, by observing Biblical examples

Preparing ourselves, and *embracing ourselves* with *courage*, through *the example* of *those* who *walked ahead of us*, is *essential* to *persevere* and to *succeed*.

For *the purpose*, of *preparing us* for the *journey ahead* of us, I *share* about *these trials*, with you. *Beyond* the *excitement* of *being involved* in *something great*, there is the *sobering reality*, of *the real challenges* we *face*, in *moving people forward*.

We *frequently read*, how the *apostle Paul encourages believers*, and *his disciples*, to *endure hardship*. *Hardship* can come in *many forms*. It *could be*, the *challenges you face*, for *doing what God called* you to *do*, or *challenges*, from those, who *oppose the message*, you bring.

Jesus faced every *conceivable kind of challenge* possible, *whilst discipling*, His *disciples*. *He was questioned many times*, He was *betrayed, deserted, accused*, and *those closest* to *Him, denied* that they even *knew Him*. Now this might *seem like an easy one* to *deal with*, *until it happens* to *you*.

The *purpose* of this *session* is to *bring us* to the *sobering reality* that, *what Jesus endured*, from *His Disciples*, is *no different, from what we might endure*, from *our disciples*, *not to speak of* what *we might endure*, from *those in the world*. *We* are *not better*, or *bigger*, than *our Master*.

> *John 15:20 (NIV) 20 Remember what I told you: 'A servant is not greater than his master.' If they persecuted me, they will persecute you also. If they obeyed my teaching, they will obey yours also.*

Let us now look at a number of challenges, all of us, will most certainly face, in our journey with Christ.

Betrayal

We might *experience, betrayal*, from *those*, in *whom we invested, hours* and *days*. *Judas betrayed Jesus. His betrayal* of the Lord is *possibly the ultimate example* of *betrayal. Jesus invested 3 and a half years*, into *disci-*

pling him, and then *he went* and *betrayed* his *Master, Friend,* and *Teacher*.

One of the *challenges with betrayal* is, that *you share your life,* with *those you disciple,* and *then they share* things, *you shared confidentially* with them, *personal things, out of context,* with *people* who *are opposed to you.* The very *things you shared in confidence,* are *shared without sentiment,* or *discretion,* with *others. This hurt!* It is *painful* to *go through betrayal,* since it is *a betrayal of trust.*

Jesus went through betrayal.

Matthew 27:3-5 (NIV) 3 When Judas, who had betrayed him, saw that Jesus was condemned, he was seized with remorse and returned the thirty pieces of silver to the chief priests and the elders. 4 "I have sinned,"
he said, "for I have betrayed innocent blood." "What is that to us?" they replied. "That's your responsibility." 5 So Judas threw the money into the temple and left. Then he went away and hanged himself.

Even though *Judas was remorseful, the consequences* of *his betrayal impacted Jesus' life, adversely. Betrayal* will *impact your life* as well.

Is there something we could do to avoid it?

The short answer is: *"Unfortunately not."* We are *facing* the *Evil one daily,* and *his attacks* come *against us* in many *different ways.* All *we can do* is, to *daily pray* for *God's Protection,* the *Grace to persevere,* and *Strength to endure,* such hostilities against us.

This challenge finds its root, in the heart of another. *Nothing you do, or say, could* really *divert* this *challenge,* unless, of course, *if you refrain* from *sharing your life* with *anyone.*

My *prayer for you* is, that *God will protect* you, and your *family, when you endure* such *viciousness.* I also *pray* that *God will help* you, to *guard your heart* against, *becoming disillusioned* and *bitter.* Remember, there was *still another eleven,* who *benefitted,* and *ultimately, took* the *message of Jesus* to the *world. Keep* your *heart focused,* towards *those* who are *with you.*

Another area, where *we could be challenged,* is *when arguments break out between our disciples.*

Arguing, disputes and disagreements

One of the things, the *enemy uses to disrupt* our *stride,* is when *he manages,* to *cause disagreements* to occur, that *results in quarrels, disputes, disagreements* and *arguments. Arguments* could *erupt against you,* or *amongst those you Disciple,* or *amongst the group* you *lead.*

Jesus' Disciples argued amongst themselves

On *one occasion, Jesus' Disciples argued among themselves* about, *who was the most important.* This is *so typical,* that *disciples* start to *compete for our affection, approval* and *affirmation.* They *often make moves* to *determine their seniority within* the *group.* This *jockeying,* to *be the closest,* and *most trusted* in the *group,* often *causes* unnecessary *strife.*

> *Mark 9:33-34 (NIV) 33 They came to Capernaum. When he was in the house, he asked them, "What were you arguing about on the road?" 34 But they kept quiet because on the way they had argued about who was the greatest.*

This *not only causes strife amongst* the *disciples,* but *also to the leader* who *needs to address it,* to *restore soundness* and *wholesome relationships* and *fellowship* amongst the disciples. *None of us like* to be *engaged in arguments* or be in the *company* of *those who constantly argue, dispute* and *disagree* with *everything and everyone.*

Sometimes there are people who engage you and make you the object of their arguments.

Arguments against you

Arguments might be brought *against you. Moses* is one of the *greatest examples,* to us, of *someone* who *endured* a *lot of arguments against him.*

He was leading Israel, out of Egypt, *to* the *land God promised* to give them as *an inheritance, yet,* they *complained,* and *grumbled,* against him *all the way.*

> *Exodus 16:2-3 (NIV) 2 In the desert **the whole community grumbled against Moses** and Aaron. 3 The Israelites said to them, "If only we had died by the LORD's hand in Egypt! There we sat around pots of meat and ate all the food we wanted, but you have brought us out into this desert to starve this entire assembly to death."*

The *Israelites apposed* the *appointments Moses made.* It almost seemed that, *regardless* of the *decision Moses* would *make, they will complain* and *grumble against it. This* was *the case* with the *appointment of Aaron,* as *High priest.*

> *Numbers 16:3 (NIV) 3 **They came as a group to oppose Moses** and Aaron and said to them, "**You have gone too far!** The whole community is holy, every one of them, and the LORD is with them. **Why then do you set yourselves above the LORD's assembly?"***

On one occasion, *their impatience* got the *better of them,* and *they* again *started* to *grumble against Moses,* because of all *the unfortunate things* they *had to endure,* along *the way to* the *Promised land.*

> *Numbers 21:4-5 (NIV) 4 They traveled from Mount Hor along the route to the Red Sea, to go around Edom. But **the people grew impatient on the way; 5 they spoke against God and against Moses,** and said, "Why have you brought us up out of Egypt to die in the wilderness? There is no bread! There is no water! And we detest this miserable food!"*

This *kind of challenge,* seem to *always* be *directed, directly to those who lead,* and *make* the *hard decisions.*

Stephen, a Believer, whom we read about in the *Book of Acts*, *encountered* this *kind of vicious attack* on him, and that, *while testifying* about his *faith in Jesus Christ*. The *arguing*, and opposition against him, *led to him* being *stoned to death*.

> Acts 6:9-10 (NIV) 9 **Opposition arose**, *however, from members of the Synagogue of the Freedmen (as it was called)—Jews of Cyrene and Alexandria as well as the provinces of Cilicia and Asia —who began to argue with Stephen. 10 But they could not stand up against the wisdom the Spirit gave him as he spoke.*

None of us are above the *possibility* of *having arguments* raised *against us*. It is in the, *how we respond to them*, that *makes the difference*. *Most of us*, in our carnal nature, *want to react*, *when arguments* are *raised against us*, however, *we learn* from these *godly men*, how to *rather respond*, and *meet the challenge*, with *faith* and by *dealing graciously*. *We can learn a lot* from *Stephen's story*, that, *even under such extra-ordinary circumstances*, he had the *faith* to continue *to witness*, and *pray* for their *pardoning, before giving up* his *spirit*.

Is there something we can do to avoid it?

The short answer is: "*No, not really, unless you don't engage people at all, on behalf of Christ.*" The *moment you act on, doing*, and *implementing instructions* from *God*, you *become an open target*, for this *kind of assault on you*, as *a person*.

How can we best deal with arguments, disputes and disagreements?

The *most expedient way* in *dealing* with this *kind of challenge*, is by being, *prayerfully considered* in your *response*. Moses frequently cried out to God, when the people argued with him. He seemed, to *1. First, hear the people out*, then *2. Speak to God*, and then *3. Respond to the people*. This *necessitates* that *we keep*, and *maintain*, a *constant walk* with the *Holy Spirit. Our preparedness, through* the *Holy Spirit,* will also *keep us* on a *good footing, when we* are about to *encounter* such *opposition* from the *Evil one.*

Another, most *expedient way,* in *dealing with* this kind of *attack,* is of course, to *not make,* or take *it personal.* Unless you did something really stupid, and deserve to have arguments raised against you, see it for what it is. *It is a spiritual attack,* most of the times. The *Bible* rightly *teaches* us in this regard.

> *Ephesians 6:12 (NIV)*
> *12 For our struggle is not against flesh and blood, but against the rulers, against the authorities, against the powers of this dark world and against the spiritual forces of evil in the heavenly realms.*

Another area, where *we are challenged* with *our disciples,* is when *they, unexpectedly, make as if* they *don't know us,* nor, *are* closely *connected to us.* We call it, *Denying.*

Denying

Sometimes, *we invest* in *people's lives,* for *years,* and then, through *some incident,* they *part ways without resolve.* Then, *when* you *see them again,* they *either make out* as if *they don't know you,* or *never met you* before, *especially in front* of *strangers.* The *self-communication,* to *remain positive,* and *sound thinking,* could *sometimes* be *quite challenging.*

Jesus experienced this with Peter

Jesus had this *infamous experience, with Peter,* where *he denied knowing Jesus.* From *all accounts, Peter* appeared to be *one* of the *three closest Disciples. Had* it *not been,* that *Jesus foretold Peter* of him *denying him, three times,* this *would have* really been *an extremely disappointing experience* for *Jesus.* The *Bible recounts* this *story.*

*John 18:25-27 (NIV) 25 Meanwhile, Simon **Peter** was still standing there warming himself. So **they asked him**, "You aren't one of his disciples too, are you?" He denied it, saying, "I am not." 26 One of the high priest's servants, a relative of the man whose ear Peter had cut off, **challenged him**, "Didn't I see you with him in the garden?" 27 **Again Peter denied it**, and at that moment a rooster began to crow.*

Even though Jesus knew that **Peter** would **deny Him**, I have **no doubt**, that He **still felt** deep **disappointment.**

How do we deal with it, when people deny knowing us?

We can't determine how **others behave** or **respond** to **us**. As **disappointing**, and **incomprehensible** it might **seem**, that people, whom we **invested our lives into**, would **deny knowing us**, or **acknowledging us. We should never allow** their **actions**, to **leave us bitter or hurt**. It is **normal** to **be disappointed**, and **even be disillusioned** by **their treatment** of **us**, however, **leave the pain** of **rejection**, at the **feet of Jesus.**

Most of these experiences happen, once disciples transfer their affections away from you.

Another area, where **we are challenged** with our disciples, is **when they** choose to **question every word, we teach them.**

Questioning

Questioning could be **a pleasant experience, or** it might **leave you feeling interrogated** and **intimidated.** The **difference is determined,** by the **attitude** and **heart,** with **which** we **are questioned.**

When **Jesus' Disciples questioned Him**, it **came** with a true **sense** of, **wanting to learn, from** their **Master.**

*Luke 11:1 (NIV) 1 One day **Jesus was praying** in a certain place. When he finished, one of **his disciples said to him,** "Lord, **teach us to pray**, just as John taught his disciples."*

The times, when our disciples come to us, saying: *"please teach me How to,"* are those times, when we *thank the Lord* for the *privilege,* to be *able to be an instrument,* in *His Hands,* to *equip His people.* This is not a challenge, but a joy.

It *was quite a different story* when the *Sadducees and Pharisees questioned Jesus,* it *came from* their *sense of superiority* in *knowledge,* and at the *same time,* from *their feeling of insecurity, since Jesus taught* with *Power,* and with *Signs and Wonders,* which was *foreign* to *their hypocritical life examples.*

On *one* of *those occasions,* the *Teachers of the Law* and *Pharisees,* brought *a woman caught in adultery,* to Him. *They questioned Him,* but *this questioning,* was to *set him up, to denounce* the *requirements of the law. Jesus saw through* their deceitful *scheme.* Let's look at this story.

John 8:3-11 (NIV) 3 The teachers of the law and the Pharisees brought in a woman caught in adultery. They made her stand before the group 4 and said to Jesus, "Teacher, this woman was caught in the act of adultery. 5 In the Law Moses commanded us to stone such women. Now what do you say?" 6 They were using this question as a trap, in order to have a basis for accusing him. But Jesus bent down and started to write on the ground with his finger. 7 When they kept on questioning him, he straightened up and said to them, "Let any one of you who is without sin be the first to throw a stone at her." 8 Again he stooped down and wrote on the ground. 9 At this, those who heard began to go away one at a time, the older ones first, until only Jesus was left, with the woman still standing there. 10 Jesus straightened up and asked her, "Woman, where are they? Has no one condemned you?" 11 "No one, sir," she said. "Then neither do I condemn you," Jesus declared. "Go now and leave your life of sin."

To traverse between the landmines and traps, when our adversaries question us, *requires grace,* and *being led* by the *Holy Spirit,* to *provide suitable,* and *God-honoring answers,* and *outcomes. May God* always *help* and *guide you* through those terrible, *questioning times.*

On *another occasion,* the *Sadducees questioned Jesus* about the *Resurrection. This kind* of *questioning* is *not to learn* something, but *rather* as a *trap*, to *let him make a judgement*, on which they *can bring accusation,* against him.

> *Matthew 22:28-30 (NIV) 28 Now then,* ***at the resurrection, whose wife will she be of the seven, since all of them were married to her?"*** *29 Jesus replied, "You are in error because you do not know the Scriptures or the power of God. 30 At the resurrection people will neither marry nor be given in marriage; they will be like the angels in heaven.*

Jesus answered their foolishness by drawing their attention to what Scripture teaches. It is essential that we know the Scriptures, so that we may be able to answer everyone.

On another occasion ***they questioned his authority.***

> *Luke 20:2 (NIV) 2 "Tell us,* ***by what authority you are doing these things,"*** *they said. "Who gave you this authority?"*

These are extreme examples, but *essential to discuss* and *explore*, since *all of us will encounter them* to some *extent. People* will *bring unexpected questions* to *throw you offside. Others* will *question your authority, especially* when *you bring correction. Some* will *question* the *validity* of *what you belief, especially* by *those who think they know more,* because of their *"researched knowledge"* on *Google*, where *anyone* with *two fingers,* and *can type,* can *post their unfounded,* and *untested theories.*

Do not be intimidated by their *ill-founded statements of belief,* rather *defuse it,* as far as possible, by *asking* to *discuss it later.* As *far as possible, give yourself time,* to *gather your thoughts, prior to speaking* to them. *Don't be intimidated* by them. *If required, ask* your *Discipler* for *help and guidance.*

> *Colossians 4:6 (NIV) 6 Let your conversation be always full of grace, seasoned with salt,* ***so that you may know how to answer everyone.***

Another challenging situation, we *might encounter* with disciples, is that *they might desert us, leave us,* or *unexpectedly take their absence of leave,* from us. We are talking about *being deserted.*

Deserted

None of us, want to *be deserted* by *people* in whom *we invested time and effort.* In fact, *the more effort* and *time we spent* on *people,* the *more acute* we *experience the rejection of being deserted,* when it *happens.*

Jesus experienced this *in his ministry,* when some of his *disciples, deserted Him.* At one point during His ministry, many disciples, who were following him, suddenly left him. They felt that the requirements He demanded, became too demanding, to the commitment they made to follow Him. This must have been a huge challenge for Jesus.

> *John 6:60-61 (NIV) 60 On hearing it, many of his disciples said, "This is a hard teaching. Who can accept it?" 61 Aware that his disciples were grumbling about this, Jesus said to them, "Does this offend you?*
>
> *John 6:66-69 (NIV) 66 From this time many of his disciples turned back and no longer followed him. 67 "You do not want to leave too, do you?" Jesus asked the Twelve. 68 Simon Peter answered him, "Lord, to whom shall we go? You have the words of eternal life. 69 We have come to believe and to know that you are the Holy One of God."*

Peter's words must have *come as a huge relieve,* after so many *deserted Jesus,* at this stage, of *their discipleship journey.*

When does this happen?

We often find this *same phenomenon,* when *we disciple.* There *comes a point,* when *the reality,* of *what our disciples signed up* for, *hits home,* and *then,* they *just want out. Some discuss it* with you, but *most just disappear* off the scene, *too embarrassed to explain,* or *too confronted* with *their own inability,* to *grow through* the *discomfort,* that *transfor-*

mation requires. *Discipleship* is *about being transformed* into the *likeness of Christ*, and *that journey, confronts many* of *our inconsistencies*, our *worldly beliefs, habits* and *practices*.

During Jesus' final hours, all His *Disciples deserted Him,* and *fled*. It is *often, when we need* the *companionship,* of *our disciples most*, that *they leave us*. It *must have been devastating* for *Jesus*.

> *Matthew 26:56 (NIV) 56 But this has all taken place that the writings of the prophets might be fulfilled." Then all the disciples deserted him and fled.*

It is a *very real challenge,* that *we all face* in our *discipleship journey* with *our disciples,* that *one day, they too might* suddenly, and *unexpectedly, leave us, desert* us, and *just disappear, without* giving a *reason*, or *telling us why* they left.

This is a *very challenging* thing to *experience, when we disciple*. It is *wise to remember,* that *the Discipleship journey,* is *a designed program by God*, to *make us obedient* followers *of Him*.

The *discipleship journey* is *designed, to challenge* people *out of darkness into the light, out* of *ignorance to knowing, out of worldliness* into *godliness, out of passivity* into *activity*, from *spectator to practitioner*, from *a hearer to a doer*, from *disobedience to obedience*. This *process challenges* people, *out of* what is *comfortable*, into *walking by faith*.

Sometimes *the pressure,* or the *reality of the journey, overwhelms people*. On the *first Missionary journey* of the *Apostle Paul*, they *encountered* one *major demonic attack* from a *Sorcerer,* by the name of *Bar-Jesus*. The *attack came, while* they were *busy, sharing* the *Word of God* to *Sergius Paulus*, the *Proconsul in Paphos*. This attack from the Evil one, and the ensuing response of Paul, must have been *too confronting* for *John Mark*, to see *Paul declaring blindness* over Bar-Jesus, even though the *Proconsul got saved*, since we see that John *left the team straightaway*, after *this encounter*.

> *Acts 13:13 (NIV) 13 From Paphos, Paul and his companions sailed to Perga in Pamphylia, where John left them to return to Jerusalem.*

At *some later stage*, he *wanted to come back*, but *Paul did not think it wise*, since *he deserted* them *previously*.

> *Acts 15:37-40 (NIV) 37 Barnabas wanted to take John, also called Mark, with them, 38 but Paul did not think it wise to take him, because he had deserted them in Pamphylia and had not continued with them in the work. 39 They had such a sharp disagreement that they parted company. Barnabas took Mark and sailed for Cyprus, 40 but Paul chose Silas and left, commended by the believers to the grace of the Lord.*

The *reality is*, that sometimes we *have team members*, who *suddenly take their leave*, even *in the midst of campaigns* or *outreaches*. *Be prepared*, *none of us can determine*, the *multitude of things*, that *might be stirred* up *in people*, to *come to a place*, where *they suddenly desert you*, and *your efforts*, *to disciple them*.

Keep a sober perspective on your own part

It is *not all about you*, *although we* have to always *keep ourselves assessed* before the Lord, as to *how our actions*, and *behaviour*, *might have caused* the *weak*, to *leave*. *If you are the cause*, then *make amends*, at all *costs*. *Jesus trusted you* with *His sheep: make right what you did wrong*.

However, in the *same breath* I want to say: *People are complex beings*, and a *myriad of things* might have *happened*, to *make them leave*. It might *not even all bad*. Sometimes, *it is outside interferences*, *outside of their* and *our control*, that *caused them to leave*.

When it happens, make every effort to *try and connect. Err rather*, by *taking a positive approach* to their departure, *assuming* that *it's not you*, *or them*, but some *outside influence*, that *caused them to leave* so unexpectedly. *Offer words of encouragement*, *express your faith* in them, and that *you hope* they will *get through this fine. People fall ill*, suddenly *lose a family* member through *death*, unexpectedly *lose their job*, or even a *natural disaster* might *impact people*, to such an *extent*, that they *see no alternative*, but *to take their leave*, or *engagement with you*.

So, how do we deal with these challenges?

How did Jesus deal with these challenges while Discipling his disciples? *What kept Him going? Jesus kept His eyes on the purpose* for *which He came*, which was to die on the cross for our sins.

*Hebrews 12:2 (NIV) 2 fixing our eyes on Jesus, the pioneer and perfecter of faith. For the joy set before him **he endured the cross, scorning its shame, and sat down at the right hand of the throne of God.***

- **Fix your eyes on Jesus!**

The advice that the Apostle offers us here in Hebrews is to fix our eyes on Jesus, and not throw away our confidence in God, and by faith trust that He who Promised, will fulfill His promises.

- **God will finish what He started!**

Paul exhorts us in the Book of Philippians to persevere in doing the will of God, since He who started this good work in us will continue to finish His work.

*Philippians 1:6 (NIV) 6 being confident of this, that **he who began a good work** in you **will carry it on to completion** until the day of Christ Jesus.*

When discipling people, who are human, we sometimes forget that they are in this discipling relationship with us, because of some supernatural miracle that happened with them. Remember, that it because of what Jesus did in their lives, that we have this privileged relationship with them.

We also forget that it is God who works in us, by His Holy Spirit. It is not all about you, and your seemingly failed, or successful efforts. It has always been the work of God. Our part has always been, that of being committed, to providing a godly example, for them to follow, and to work, to see Christ formed in them. Anything more, or anything other than this pure motive, would not be from God.

> *Hebrews 10:35 (NIV) 35 So **do not throw away your confidence**; it will be richly rewarded. 36 **You need to persevere** so that when you have done the will of God, **you will receive what he has promised.***

We are encouraged to not "***shrink back.***"

> *Hebrews 10:39 (NIV) 39 But **we do not belong to those who shrink back** and are destroyed, but to those who have faith and are saved.*

Action Steps

How to Prepare to endure these Trials

Here are a few lessons we have learnt along the path of seeing Disciples multiply. I learned a valuable lesson, from a variety of articles I read, about men and women, who did extraordinary things in their lives.

1. Be Mentally and Spiritually Prepared

The story of Sir Edmund Hillary and his incredible success, becoming the first person to summit Mount Everest in Nepal in 1953, teaches us the incredible lesson of succeeding through the most extreme and exhausting circumstances. One of the key reasons he was successful is because he prepared himself spiritually and mentally. After a few failed attempts, he went more spiritually and physically prepared, and then did.

We will be wise if we continue on this discipling journey with open eyes, soberness, and prepared to deal with these challenges before they happen, and seeing our disciples become fruitful and multiply.

In Hebrews 11, the writer records the names of people who paid a high price for the spreading of the message of Hope. They encouraged each other with what they knew, so they could endure any challenges, they faced.

2. Be prepared to lose

It might cost you your reputation, position or confidence! It is important that we are aware that discipling people comes at a price. It is a high price that might cost you everything you have. This was true for the apostles and it may be true for us. Since we died with Christ, let us live our lives in full surrender to His Will, and that, in one sense, is taking up our cross daily.

*Mark 8:34-38 (KJV), "And when he had called the people unto him with his disciples also, he said unto them, **whosoever** will come after me, **let him deny himself, and take up his cross, and follow me.***

Christ made himself *"**nothing**"* that He might serve us.

*Philippians 2:5, 7 (NIV) 5 In your relationships with one another, have the same mindset as Christ Jesus: 7 rather, he made himself nothing by **taking the very nature of a servant**, being made in human likeness.*

Discipling others requires humility at the best of times. We need to always remember that we are here to serve them.

3. The more prepared you are before your start the better you will endure the challenges.

If we prepare ourselves to face these challenges, beforehand, we will be more prepared to overcome them.

I pray that you will be better equipped through this session, and I pray that you will keep the Word of God close to your heart as you too endure the many obstacles that we will face. Finally, always remind your disciples that we do all of this for the King. This brings us to rewards.

Which are the areas where you are challenged in at the moment?

_____

_____

_____

What steps will you take to counter, or deal with these challenges? _____

_____

_____

_____

What is that one Scripture that you will make your own as you face these challenges? _____

_____

11

ETERNAL REWARDS

We will *all stand before the Lord* and *give account of ourselves* before *him. This session* is *about* drawing our attention to this *fact*, that *we will all stand before God*, to *give account* of the *work He assigned* to *each of us to do.* This *session* also *serves as a reminder* that *we need to work* in *such a way* that *we will receive* a *rich reward* in *Heaven.* In *Paul's first letter* to the *church in Corinth*, he *exhorted them to build wisely*, since *their work* will be *tested by fire*, and *what remains will be rewarded. Let's look* at this *amazing portion* of *Scripture.*

> *1 Corinthians 3:10-15 (NIV) 10 By the grace God has given me, **I laid a foundation as a wise builder**, and someone else is building on it. But **each one should build with care.** 11 For no one can lay any foundation other than the one already laid, which is Jesus Christ. 12 **If anyone builds on this foundation using gold, silver, costly stones, wood, hay or straw,** 13 their work will be shown for what it is, because **the Day will bring it to light. It will be revealed with fire, and the fire will test the quality of each person's work.** 14 If what has been **built survives, the builder will receive a reward.** 15 If it is burned up, the builder will suffer loss but yet will be saved—even though only as one escaping through the flames.*

I believe *God desires* us *to build wisely.* We *can build* with *wood, hay or straw*, but *then it will* all just *be burned up. God* really *desires* that *we build with gold, silver and costly stones, so that it will withstand* the *fire test.* The *eternal rewards are reserved* for *those* who *build lasting work* on *the Foundation of Christ.*

Jesus wants us to work with Him.

In the Pastoral letter of Paul to the church in Corinth, he calls us to work, with God, as co-labourers.

> *1 Corinthians 3:8-9 (NIV) 8 The one who plants and the one who waters have one purpose, and they will each be rewarded according to their own labor. 9 For we are co-workers in God's service; you are God's field, God's building.*

Making disciples is building with gold, silver and costly stones.

Every *success stands and falls* on *our effectiveness to make disciples*, so it is *essential that we ask God for our Disciples*, and then to *disciple them well.*

Jesus once said that He *lost none of those God has given him.* This should be *our prayer* as well *daily.*

> *John 6:39 (NIV) 39 And this is the will of him who sent me, that I shall lose none of all those he has given me but raise them up at the last day.*

> *John 17:12 (NIV) 12 While I was with them, I protected them and kept them safe by that name you gave me. None has been lost except the one doomed to destruction so that Scripture would be fulfilled.*

One *prayer*, that *helps me stay focused*, and *aligned* to the *Will of God*, and *in line to receive* my *eternal reward*, is *praying* the *prayer, Jesus prayed*, in *John chapter 17.* Let us *take a few moments* to *consider this prayer* together, as we *think*, and *pray over our work,* with our *own disciples.*

> *John 17:6 (NIV) Jesus Prays for His Disciples 6 "I have revealed you to those whom you gave me out of the world. They were yours; you gave them to me, and they have obeyed your word.*

Let us consider:

1. Am I discipling, all the disciples, that God entrusted to me yet?

_____

_____

2. If not, how will you change that in His Presence today?

_____

_____

_____

3. Am I revealing you well to my disciples? _____

_____

4. Jesus often prayed for His Disciples. How often are you intentionally praying for each of your disciples? _____

> *John 17:7 (NIV) 7 Now they know that everything you have given me comes from you.*

This *Scripture speaks* to me more *about modelling,* good *stewardship,* and *practising Simplicity.*

5. Is it visibly communicated that I seek God's Kingdom first? In which way are you communicating it?

_____

_____

6. Do my disciples know that I am committed to store up in Heavenly places? How do you model it? _____

_____

_____

7. Is the way I use, and invest my resources, clearly and visibly showing my commitment, to advance the Kingdom of God? _____

8. Am I giving enough credit to God, as the source of my providence?

_____

*John 17:8 (NIV) 8 For **I gave them the words you gave me**, and **they accepted them. They knew with certainty** that I came from you, and they believed that you sent me.*

One of the ways we instil this awareness in our disciples, is by the consistency, in which we minister to them, not in the persuasion of human wisdom, but in the Power of the Holy Spirit. The Apostle Paul is such a great example to us in this matter. He affirmed this with the church in Corinth as well.

9. How intentional are you, to rely on, and minister in the power of the Holy Spirit, to your disciples? _____

_____

*1 Corinthians 2:4-5 (NIV) 4 My message and my preaching were not with wise and persuasive words, but **with a demonstration of the Spirit's power**, 5 so that **your faith might** not **rest** on human wisdom, but **on God's power**.*

This is the kind of reputation we desire with our disciples, that we give them God's Word consistently.

10. When last did you experience the Power of God, as you ministered to your disciples? What happened? _____

_____
_____
_____

*John 17:9 (NIV) 9 **I pray for them**. I am not praying for the world, but **for those you have given me**, for they are yours.*

A few times Jesus mentions that He prays for His disciples. It is of great value to mention before Father that you are praying for those entrusted to you.

11. How often do you intentionally pray for your disciples? _____

*John 17:11-12 (NIV) 11 I will remain in the world no longer, but they are still in the world, and I am coming to you. **Holy Father, protect them** by the power of your name, the name you gave me, so **that they may be one as we are one**. 12 While I was with them, **I protected them** and **kept them safe** by that name you gave me. **None has been lost** except the one doomed to destruction so that Scripture would be fulfilled.*

***Protecting** our **Disciples is important** to **Jesus**.* In the same way as, what Jesus prayed for the protection of his disciples, we need to pray for the protection of our disciples. Let us take a few moments now and pray for our disciples. Take time, on each of these points.

- Pray for the physical protection
- Pray for their spiritual protection from the evil one.
- Pray for protection of false doctrines.
- Pray for protection for their disciples and those they are pursuing to reach for Christ.
- Pray that the seed of the Word be protected that Satan will not steal it, or destroy it, but that it will accomplish everything for which it was purposed. May the Word, sown in their lives, not return back void.

*John 17:14-15 (NIV) 14 **I have given them your word** and the world has hated them, for **they are not of the world any more** than I am of the world. 15 **My prayer is** not that you take them out of the world but **that you protect them from the evil one**.*

The ***moment** we **start sharing** the **Word of God**, or **start reaching out** to **people around us**, we **will encounter opposition**, from Satan. **People will hate** you and **persecute you**. **We need to pray** for the **protection** of* *our disciples. May the Lord protect them emotionally, and mentally, when they are harassed.*

> *John 17:17, 19 (NIV) 17 Sanctify them by the truth; your word is truth. 19 For them I sanctify myself, that they too may be truly sanctified.*

One thing that we always *want to see* in our *disciples*, is the visible, *sanctification work* of the *Holy Spirit*. What *Jesus taught us* in *this prayer*, is to *continually pray*, over *our disciples*: "*Father, sanctify them with Your Word and by your Holy Spirit.*" The extent to which we, consistently pray this over our disciples, is the extent to which we will see, a sanctification work released over their lives.

12. How often do you pray for the sanctification work of the Holy Spirit over the lives of your disciples? _____

13. How can you improve on it? _____

_____

_____

> *John 17:18 (NIV) 18 As you sent me into the world, I have sent them into the world.*

We are all "*sent ones.*" The Great Commission starts with an instruction to "*GO,*" and each of us should demonstrate that we are "*going.*" We also need to "*send*" our disciples into the world, as Jesus sent His Disciples, into the world.

14. Have you considered, sending your disciples out on their God-given mission? _____

15. What "sending" will you do with your disciples, that you believe that you are already modelling to them? _____

_____

_____

The *Gospel will never grow, beyond our willingness* to "*go.*" **We need to send them!**

*Romans 10:14-15 (NIV) 14 **How, then, can they call on the one they have not believed in?** And **how can they believe** in the one of **whom they have not heard?** And **how can they hear without someone preaching to them?** 15 And **how can anyone preach unless they are sent?** As it is written: "**How beautiful are the feet of those who bring good news!**"*

The **only biblical way** is that **we need to send our Disciples,** to **go,** as *Jesus sent His.*

*John 17:20-21 (NIV) 20 "**My prayer is not for them alone. I pray also for those who will believe in me through their message,** 21 that all of them may be one, Father, just as you are in me and I am in you. **May they also be in us** so that the world may believe that you have sent me.*

What **Jesus is teaching us** here, is that **we,** not only need to **pray for our disciples,** when they go, but also **pray for those** who **will hear their message. We pray,** that **God** will **open their hearts,** to **receive Him.**

16. How often do you pray, for those, to whom your disciples are ministering? _____

17. What action steps, can you take, to better put this, prayer example of Jesus, into practice, in your own prayer life? _____

_____

_____

_____

_____

_____

*John 17:25-26 (NIV) 25 "Righteous Father, though the world does not know you, **I know you,** and they know that you have sent me. 26 **I have made you known to them, and will continue to make you known** in order that **the love you have for me may be in them** and that **I myself may be in them.**"*

The extent to which we, ourselves, are invested in this process of *making Christ Known, is the extent* to which our disciples, *will make Christ known*, as well.

Closing remarks

In closing, I want to *encourage and remind you* of the *Abrahamic Promise* and *Blessing over your life*:

> *Genesis 12:2-3 (NIV) 2 "I will make you into a great nation, and I will bless you; I will make your name great, and you will be a blessing. 3 I will bless those who bless you, and whoever curses you I will curse; and all peoples on earth will be blessed through you.*

> *Genesis 17:4-6 (NIV) 4 "As for me, this is my covenant with you: You will be the father of many nations. 5 No longer will you be called Abram; your name will be Abraham, for I have made you a father of many nations. 6 I will make you very fruitful; I will make nations of you, and kings will come from you.*

> *Genesis 18:18-19 (NIV) 18 Abraham will surely become a great and powerful nation, and all nations on earth will be blessed through him. 19 For I have chosen him, so that he will direct his children and his household after him to keep the way of the LORD by doing what is right and just, so that the LORD will bring about for Abraham what he has promised him."*

Within *these* few *records*, of *when God spoke to Abraham*, we *have record of the Blessing,* with which *God blessed Abraham, and all of us who believe. This promise is for you,* and *your spiritual children.* This is *my prayer for you*: that *you will be fruitful,* and *multiply greatly*; that *you will be a Father of Nations,* and *that Nations will be blessed through you. Choose well,* and *equip well!*
God bless you!

12

OTHER BOOKS BY DR HENDRIK J VORSTER

Step One - Salvation

This Course explores the "How to" be Born Again and to establish a solid Foundation for your faith in Jesus Christ. It is based on Hebrews chapter 6 verses 1 and 2, and explores:

Repentance of dead works,

Faith in God,

Baptisms,

Laying on of hands,

Resurrection of the dead, and

Eternal Judgement

Discipleship Foundations - Step One - Salvation Disciple Manual

Teacher Manuals and Video Teaching material are available through our website: www.churchplantinginstitute.com

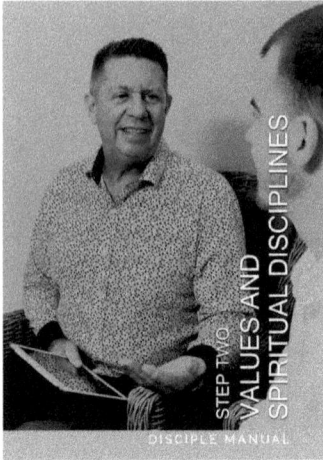

Discipleship Foundations Step Two - Values and Spiritual Disciplines Disciple Manual

Step Two - Values and Spiritual Disciplines Disciple Manual

This Course explores the "How to" develop spiritual disciplines as well as 52 Values Jesus taught. It is based on the teachings of Jesus to His Disciples, and explores:

Spiritual Disciplines

The disciplines we explore are: Reading, meditating on the Word of God, Prayer, Stewardship, Fasting, Servanthood, Simplicity, Worship, and Witnessing.

Values of the Kingdom of God

Humility, Mournfulness, meekness, Spiritual Passion, Mercifulness, Purity, Peacemaker, Patient endurance, Example, Custodian, Reconciliatory, Resoluteness, Loving, Discreetness, Forgiving, Kingdom of God Investor, God-minded, Kingdom of God prioritiser, Introspective, Persistent, Considerate, Conservative, Fruit-bearing, Practitioner, Accountability, Faithful, Childlikeness, Unity, Servanthood, Loyalty, Gratefulness, Stewardship, Obedience, Carefulness, Compassion, Caring, Confidence, Steadfastness, Contentment, Teachable, Deference, Diligence, Trustworthiness, Gentleness, Discernment, Truthfulness, Generous, Kindness, Watchfulness, Perseverance, Honouring and Submissive.

Teacher Manuals and Video Teaching material are available through our website: www.churchplantinginstitute.com

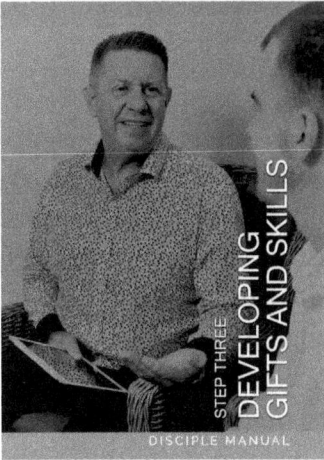

Discipleship Foundations Step Three - Developing Gifts and Skills

Step Three - Developing Gifts and Skills

This course is run through five weekend encounters. These weekend encounters have been designed to help Disciples discover their spiritual gifts, as well as learn skills to use their gifts, and to serve the Lord for the extension of His Kingdom. The Weekend Encounters are:

Gifts Discovery Weekend Encounter

We learn about Ministerial Office gifts, Service gifts, and Supernatural Spiritual Gifts. We discover our own, and then learn How we may use them to build up the local Church.

Survey of the Bible Weekend Encounter

During this weekend we do a survey of the Bible, from Genesis to Revelation. We also learn about the History of the Bible as well as How we can make most of our time in the Word.

Sharing your Faith Weekend Encounter

During this weekend we learn about the Gospel message, and How to share our faith effectively.

Overcoming Weekend Encounter

During this weekend we deal with those thistles and thorns that smother the growth and harvest of the good seed sown into our lives. We address How to overcome fear, unforgiveness, lust and the cares of the world with faith and obedience.

Shepherd Leader Weekend Encounter

During this weekend encounter we learn about being a Good Shepherd, and How to best disciple in a small group.

Teacher Manuals and Video Teaching material are available from our website: www.churchplantinginstitute.com

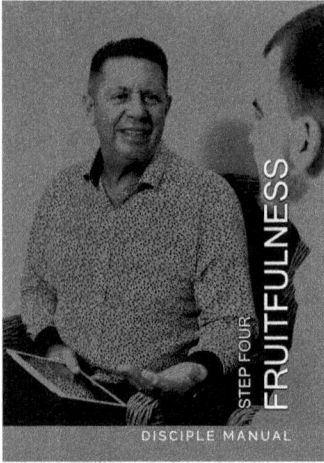

Discipleship Foundations Step Four - Fruitfulness

Step Four - Discipling Fruit-Producers

We were saved to serve. This course has been designed to mobilise Believers, from Learners to Practitioners. These sessions have been prepared for individual use, with those who are bearing fruit, and want to produce more fruit. Developing these areas in a sustained and systematic manner will ensure both fruitfulness and multiplication. Attending to these areas will ensure that you bear lasting fruit.

We explore:

1. Introduction.
2. Walking with purpose.
3. Build purposeful relationships. Finding Worthy Men
4. Priesthood. Praying effectively for those entrusted to you.
5. Caring compassionately.
6. Walking worthily.
7. Walking in the Spirit.
8. Practicing hospitality.

Teacher Manuals and Video Teaching material are available from our COURSES link from our website at:

www.churchplantinginstitute.com

Step Five - Multiplication

This course was designed to assist fruit-producing disciples to live a life that will encourage a lifetime of fruitfulness. It will also give our disciples skills and guidelines to navigate their disciples through seasons of challenge and growth. This course is packed with Leadership advancing principles. The more these areas are addressed and encouraged, the more we will experience growth and multiplication. We explore:

1. Vision and dreams.
2. Set Godly Goals.
3. Character development
4. Gifts development - Impartation and Activation
5. Fruitfulness comes through constant challenge.
6. Relationships - Family, Children and Friends
7. The Power of encouragement
8. Finances - Personal and Ministry finances
9. Dealing with setbacks

- How to deal with failure?
- How to deal with betrayal?
- How to deal with rejection?
- How to deal with trials?
- How to deal with despondency?

10. Eternal rewards

Teacher Manuals and Video Teaching material are available from our website: www.churchplantinginstitute.com

Values
of the
Kingdom
of
God

Dr. Hendrik J. Vorster

Values of the Kingdom of God
By Dr. Hendrik J Vorster

Everyone desires to be known as a pleasant to be around with kind of person. This book helps you develop values towards such a godly character. This book explores 52 Values of the Kingdom of God.

Books are available from our website: www.churchplantinginstitute.com

SPIRITUAL
DISCIPLINES
OF THE
KINGDOM
OF
GOD

Spiritual Disciplines of the Kingdom of God
By Dr. Hendrik J Vorster

Every Believer desires to be a Fruit-producing branch in the Vineyard of our Lord. Developing spiritual disciplines is to develop spiritual roots from which our faith can draw sap to grow strong and fruit-bearing branches. This Book explores Nine Spiritual Disciplines of the Kingdom of God.

Books are available from our website: www.churchplantinginstitute.com

Church Planting

How to plant a dynamic church

Dr. Hendrik J. Vorster

Foreword by: Dr. Yonggi Cho

Church Planting - by Dr Hendrik J Vorster

Church Planting - How to plant a dynamic, disciple-making church

By Dr Hendrik J Vorster

This is a handbook for those who wish to plant a disciple-making church. This book explores every aspect of church planting, and is widely used in over 70 Nations on 6 Continents. Here is a list of the areas that are explored:

1. The challenge to plant New Churches
2. Phases of Church Planting
3. Phase One of Church Planting - The Calling, Vision and Preparation Phase
4. The Call to Church Planting
5. Twelve Characteristics of Church Planting Leaders
6. Church Planting Terminology
7. Phase Two of Church Planting - Discipleship
8. The Process of Discipleship
9. Phase Three of Church Planting - Congregating the Discipleship Groups
10. Understanding Church Planting Finances
11. Understanding Church staff
12. Phase Four of Church Planting - Ministry development and Church Launching Phase
13. Understanding and Implementing Systems
14. Phase Five of Church Planting - Multiplication
15. Understanding the challenges in Church Planting
16. How to succeed in Church Planting
17. How to plant a House Church

Student Manuals and Video Teaching material are available from our website: www.churchplantinginstitute.com